Just Shellfish

Gary the Lemon Cheesecake

This is a work of fiction. Names, characters, places, and incidents either are the product of the author's imagination or are used fictitiously. Any resemblance to actual persons, living or dead, events, locales or cheesecakes is entirely coincidental.

First edition 2025

ISBN: 9798275486544

Content Warning: Just *Shellfish is a work of tragicomic psychological horror that contains graphic and mature themes. It is intended for adult readers, including themes of mental health issues, suicide, isolation, sexual objectification and anxiety. The narrative is an exploration of trauma and mental health, with themes that may be disorienting or distressing for some readers.*

"I keep you safe you shellfish git, from cults and plots and other shit" —Billby the Bear

Prologue

Billby here.

Right then. You read the synopsis? Good.

What's that? Couldn't find it? Course you didn't. Lazy git. It was barely ten words mate. You even look? Fine, here's the short version: Prawn's in danger, the shellfish sod. I'm the one who keeps him safe from the cult conspiracy he's found himself tied up in, probably literally at the rate he's going. I'm bloody hilarious, by the way, but this is no joke.

Now can we get on with it already? He's about to order a pizza and I can already tell this is going to go swimmingly.

Try to keep up, won't you?

All my love,

Billby the Bear

Chapter 1 - Nitwit

"Look, Mr Stevens. You say it's fraud, but the address matches yours, you made a payment shortly after this one, and the timeline you've given me just isn't consistent with the details we hold on file."

I let that hang there, give him some time to stew. Silence brought truth more often than any facts or figures I could present. Seconds stretched before he finally responded.

"I just—my daughter really wanted it. Apple of my eye, mate, and she eyed up that laptop and... bloody hell. Wife's gonna kill me. But I really need the money back..."

Unfortunately for this joker, we refund fraud, not buyer's remorse.

"You may still be able to return it to the merchant and request a refund, sir. But I'm not recommending you proceed with a fraud case at this stage, as you are incredibly likely to be declined, and it may trigger an account review."

Let that hang there too. Be smart and drop it already. Fudge.

"Guess I'm gonna have to. Thanks, Prawn. What kind of name is that anyway? I'll bet you're very shellfish!"

"Very original, sir. Have a great day."

I clicked that call into oblivion, along with my rapidly deteriorating sanity.

"You alright, Billby?"

My teddy bear was a great listener, but not much of a conversationalist. Still, nice to have someone watching over me as I worked. Somehow made me feel like less of a fraud myself.

Speaking of which, I was about to have a performance review with Sarah. Can't wait. Fudge.

Be still, beating heart. Well, not permanently, but settle down already. These always sucked.

"Peter, how are you?" Sarah said, bright and cheery-eyed for four on a Friday.

"Um, I'm fine, I guess," I mumbled.

"You've been doing great work. Top of my team, always impressed by your adherence to process and targets."

What did that even mean, anyway? Was that manager talk for 'We're onto you?'

Doubt it. But still, didn't sit right with me. Heard the words she said but didn't feel them. It was the ones she said behind my back that worried me.

"Um, thanks," I meekly offered.

"You stopped a significant first-party fraud case last week too. Office has been buzzing about you."

"Oh, um, thanks," I mumbled. All but confirmed that theory, then. Talking about me, watching me.

"You do have a remote work exception, but if you ever want to join a team meeting at the hub, we'd love to have—"

"No, no, thank you."

"That's all really then. Keep doing what you do. See you in two months for your next review!"

Well, that was that. Heart still hammering away, but I slumped in my chair and finally felt like I could breathe.

Still, last call of the day was done. I carefully took off my headset, plonked it on the desk, picked up my bear, and plonked him on my gaming desk in my living room.

With the calls out the way, it was time to go have some fun. I had a meeting scheduled with my guild leader to talk about my recent performance.

I turned on my laptop, booted up my game with a smile on my face. I didn't have to be incompetent Peter the Prawn here, I was Prawnstar, paladin of Justice and righteousness, guild officer, raid leader.

"There's my favourite Prawnstar!" Badger said, joining the call.

"Badger! My guy! How are you, mate?"

"All good, all good. So how's things? Haven't seen you online so much lately, Prawn."

"Yeah, overtime with work. Sorry, mate. Just had the worst performance review in history."

"I get it, real life can get in the way sometimes, can't it. Been struggling in the raids without our star tank, though, Prawnstar."

"Ah, no worries. I'm all good, easy, looking forward to the next one."

"Right. About that. No easy way to say this, but we're promoting Jester to officer, and you're demoted, I'm afraid."

"What! That's outrageous, mate! I'm the best tank on the team!"

Fudge! What the fudging hell! This was ridiculous. How could he do this? I was the best!

"Well, you are the most consistent, but his DPS outranks yours—and frankly, he's more available, since he's out of employment."

Bloody hell. How am I supposed to compete with that feckless jobless twit if he has all the time in the world to play? This is ridiculous. Settle down, settle down.

Billby, give me a bloody hug. I grabbed him from my gaming desk, hugged him tight against me like a shield from a snake.

3

"We're not kicking you, Prawn, but be honest with yourself. You can't keep performing with all the work you do, can you?"

Fudge. That hurt. But was he lying? Of course he was! I'm the bloody best!

"This isn't fair, Badger. I'm—I—"

Ah, what's the fudging point? He won't listen. Made up his mind, clearly—guess I'm just yesterday's news to this guild now.

"We're off to go raid the Crystal Caverns, Prawn. How about you join us, mate? We'd love to have you!"

"No, thanks. I should eat. Maybe see if there's more overtime."

"Enjoy. Later, mate."

Fudge. Not remotely fair. I deserved that officer's position and they've just taken it away from me. I worked hard for the guild, led so many raids, and they just shut me out completely like that. Yesterday's news, an old pair of dirty socks, a—

"Bunch of muppets."

Huh? What was—who said—

"Me, nitwit."

I froze. Stared deep into Billby's eyes, lifeless and still. No, teddy bears don't talk. He didn't say anything. They're inanimate objects, they—

"You're a sodding inanimate object."

Nope! Not happening! I'm just stressed. Just angry, just—

"Just bloody bonkers, mate," Billby didn't say.

"Shut up!" I yell out loud to... my bear. My stuffed, lifeless teddy bear, who definitely didn't just call me a nitwit.

"Bears don't talk, Billby. Settle down."

Silence. Nothing.

"Billby?"

4

More silence. Good, good. Fudge, that was—fudge. That was fudge.

Whatever, I need to eat something. Been a bloody stressful day, two failed competency reviews.

Right, well. Guess I'll bring up my app and order some pizza? Or... I don't know. Just food.

Hmm. Half off if I call them... Ugh. I do enough of that at work, and I'm bloody awful at it. Well, half price is half price. My hands shook a little as I tapped in the number, hit dial.

"Spicy Pizza Palace, take your order please?"

Right, right. Should have rehearsed this. No scripts or standard operating procedures for this one.

"What do you sell?" I enquire.

"Pizza?"

"Oh. Uh..."

OK, well, ask a dumb question I suppose. Right, the half-price offer. Let's enquire carefully about that.

"Price, half?"

"Sir? Try that again please."

Fudge! Just, take a breath. Stop shaking hand! Just a bloody pizza.

"Just a bloody pizza, please."

"Right, well, we don't sell them with blood, and I need to know your toppings and size."

"Size? Um... I guess I'm a medium build, I—"

"What size PIZZA, sir! Christ. They don't pay me enough for this."

Settle down there, mate. Settle down. Fudge.

"Um, cheese, please."

"Great. Size?"

"Cheese."

"Oh, for the love of—what size cheese pizza?"

"Uh, what size is suitable for a six-foot-tall man, medium build, broad shoulders—"

"Sending you the fucking medium. Anything else, mate?"

"Yes, do you sell a jar of honey, for my bear?"

Why. *Why* did I try that. Fudge. Fudgity-fudge fudge.

"What? No, of course we bloody—"

"Sorry, sorry. I was just trying to be funny."

"You couldn't possibly be any bloody funnier, mate. Half hour, twenty quid cash."

Fudge. Don't think that could possibly have gone any worse. Were my work calls all that bad? Ugh.

Well, at least I had a pizza coming to look forward to. I could already taste the peppers and the tuna. I was in for a treat.

Wait—blast. I don't think I actually mentioned those. I don't think I got the discount either! Should have just used the bloody app.

I'm cursed today, I swear. Everything I touch, or try, just going horribly wrong. Right, time to settle down, and prepare myself for the delivery guy. Took a long, deep breath and fumbled in my pocket for my wallet. Probably just going to ask for the money then vanish, which I'm more than happy with.

Really wish I had a coin to give him as a tip though. Not sure they're paid very much, especially with him driving all the way out here. Blast, could I ask a neighbour maybe?

Don't think so. Haven't spoken to one yet, where I can help it, so why start now. Too bad I can't get one from Billby. Then again, he's not exactly going to help me eat the pizza now, is he. Doubt a bear even likes peppers anyway.

"They're alright, mate," Billby didn't say.

Huh. Did—no, no.

Settle down, Prawn. Just a teddy bear. Just a pizza. Should be here in, uh... about four more minutes.

No idea why I can't stop shaking! Makes no sense—just ordering a pizza. Not doing anything wrong, not blowing up the building or starting random fires or hijacking a plane. Literally just ordering a pizza, extra peppers and tuna.

Oh, bugger. That's right. No peppers.

"No tuna either, numpty," Billby didn't mock.

Staring at his lifeless eyes, I almost felt like he was laughing with me. Or maybe at me? It was honestly hard to tell sometimes.

Two minutes. When did my hand start shaking? Better sit on the sofa, bit more comfortable, relaxing.

Fudge, I really wish I had a tip for the guy. Maybe I just offer him a slice of pizza? He delivers them all the time but does anyone ever actually offer him a slice? Doubt it.

That'll work, I think. Yeah, I'm sure it will. I can't wait to sink my teeth in, can already taste the warm dough, melted cheese and tomato.

"A plain cheese pizza, no tuna or pepper. Adventurous, mate," Billby didn't say snarkily.

I'm definitely imagining things, bloody bear. I'm just stressed, that's all. Been a day.

One minute.

I closed my eyes, took some deep breaths. Cleared a spot on the counter, had the twenty ready, he'd be here any second. I could hear his boots echoing from the hallway, getting louder and louder as he approached my door. Oh fudge, oh fudge, oh fudge. Here he is. Here we go.

"Be careful, mate."

I look around again. Alone in my flat. Just need to watch out, be polite, offer him a slice with his twenty. Nothing could possibly go wrong, just a pizza, just a slice, just dinner.

"Just bananas, mate."

Just bananas.

Chapter 2 - Stranger

Ahhh fudge. He's knocking on the door now, echoing through my very soul. So bloody loud!

Right, stick to the plan. Got the twenty, grab the pizza, offer slice, send him on his way, tuck in. Can already taste the peppers.

"No you can't," Billby didn't mock.

Right, right. Hand shaking like a maraca as I opened the door.

"Hi, mate, one medium cheese pizza?"

"Uh, yes, hi, yes. Cheese? Not pepper or tuna?"

He opened the lid to have a peek. "No, mate."

Blast. Could swear Billby was gloating just from looking over at his eyes.

"Um, thank you. Thanks, I mean. Slice?"

"Sorry?"

Oh duh, he's waiting for the note. Take a breath, settle down, focus.

"Here's the money. Um, want a slice?"

A smile spread across his face, looking up at me. He had striking green eyes from under that pizza hat he wore. Fetching.

"Get a room, mate," Billby didn't mock.

"Mate, you're a legend to offer. Nobody ever does. Heck yes, I'll have a slice."

"Great, I'll—"

Wait a minute. What—what the hell is he doing! He's inside my flat! He's INSIDE my FLAT! He's! He came in! Sofa! Fudgefudgefudge—

"Comfy sofa, mate! I'm Marcus. Come grab some pizza, then."

Better. Better not. Better had? Better had.

"Better calm down, numpty," Billby didn't prod.

Right then. Just gonna... sit next to this stranger. Stranger with the striking green emerald eyes, sat on my sofa, eating my pizza. Yep, this is fine. Fine. Perfectly fine. No issues or problems or—

"You alright there, mate? Look all sweaty. On edge, maybe. You good?"

"Oh! Yes! Emerald. Um, nice to Marcus you meet. I'm Prawn."

Marcus began to chuckle, smiling over at me. "Oh, mate, you're a riot. You a comedian or something? What's with the name Prawn then? You shellfish?"

"Not exactly bloody original, is he?" Billby didn't jab.

"Oh, um, just my initials. Peter Ross Awning."

"That's kinda cool actually, mate. Hey, thanks for my slice, Prawn, you're a good guy. See you around, maybe?"

Hell no. Helllllllll no. I'm never ordering pizza again. Ever. Never ever ever.

"Yep. Um, thanks. Take another slice for the road if you would like, I mean, to eat on the road. Don't drop it there, road isn't hungry."

Oh fudge. Bumbling bloody buggering nitwit. Settle down, Prawn.

"Oh, mate, you're hilarious! You're a top bloke. Later, Prawn," Marcus cackled as he headed out the door.

I slumped myself against it, locking it tight, finally able to breathe again. Stared over at Billby, silently judging me with his lifeless eyes. Silly bear.

"You're quiet. Nothing to add? No mockery or jabs or jibes?"

Nothing. Just stared back at me, blank as a piece of paper, as a teddy bear should. Well... guess I'll eat what's left of my pizza, but it somehow felt tainted now. Stomach in knots. No room left for pizza.

"Up you get, mate. Settle down, chin up."

Couldn't slump here forever. I dragged myself back to the sofa, carefully chewing a piece of pizza. So lifeless and dull without the peppers and tuna. Why couldn't I just have practised before ordering? Half price, medium pizza, peppers and tuna. Half price, medium pizza, peppers and tuna.

"You let a stranger into your flat. A STRANGER," Billby didn't say.

Bloody bear. Maybe I should put this pizza in the fridge and just go back to gaming. Prawnstar doesn't need to be a guild officer to have a little fun, right?

"Demoted. Deflated. Defeated."

"Shut up!" I yelled at my bear, sat there lifeless and still.

I grabbed him and gave him a hug. He isn't talking or mocking or thinking, I'm just stressed out. It hasn't been a good day today, with two horrible performance reviews, the demotion, and the whole... pizza ordeal.

"Literally just a pizza order, mate. Weren't diffusing a bomb now, were you?"

Alone in my flat again, staring at my laptop. Just not sure I could be bothered, really. I'd have to sit in a party, following orders from my replacement, false praise from Badger. Thought he was my friend.

"Out to get you, like everyone else."

Guess there was some truth to that. The demotion was proof. I deserved that, I led so many raids and in the end it meant nothing. Maybe I was a fraud all along.

"Just a game, mate, settle down."

Still, didn't need the game to have fun. Or the guild, even—plenty more I could do. Maybe see if there's any overtime available for the evening, go do some work instead.

"If that's your idea of fun mate I might need to find you a girlfriend," Billby didn't jest.

I sighed, slumped back in my sofa, staring at the spot Marcus sat in. He genuinely seemed nice, didn't he? Kind, fun—

"Strange. Unfamiliar. Dangerous."

"Not everyone is dangerous!" I snapped at my lifeless, inanimate bear.

Silence. Nice bit of peace and quiet. Might put the telly on, watch the news, but lately it's always just some tragic bullshit.

"You're tragic bullshit," Billby didn't mock.

Screw this. Think I'm just getting an early night. Gonna just slump on my bed. Nice and soft, mattress gentle against my back.

Huh, another text from Dad I don't particularly want to read. Probably just another invitation to some distant relative's birthday party that I've never met.

"Safer here."

Guess I'm just going to read it later. Maybe.

Sometimes I wish Billby was a real bear. He could help me eat the rest of the pizza.

"What even is real anyway, mate."

Not having that existential crisis at nine on a Friday night. Fudge it, crawling in bed, scrolling random videos on my phone for three hours then dozing off. Yet, found myself tapping on the text from Dad.

"You all good, son?"

How was I supposed to even respond to that? Sure, Dad, fine and dandy? I glared at the screen for a while before turning it off. Like he cared anyway, too busy gallivanting around South London, drinking his liver into Swiss cheese.

"Guilt."

Probably still blames himself for Tim. We were just kids, and he—why did—why would—

"Stop," Billby didn't say. *"Past. Future."*

Right. Eyes on the road ahead. I'm getting my guild back, and I'm finishing that pizza. I'm going to try and apply myself at work, too—the more I try the more I learn, right?

"Imposter."

Fudge.

Chapter 3 - Invaded

I used to love Saturdays, but I'm finding myself just blankly staring at my screen scrolling through a library of ninety games. Ninety games yet nothing to play. Sort of feels like I'm looking in the fridge and every shelf is full of carrots.

Checked my email, got one from Badger about a guild meeting tonight. Not sure I can be bothered, really—haven't felt like going since they demoted me.

"Shunned. Ousted."

It's fine. I'll just find a puzzle game or something instead, or maybe actually call someone?

Nah. Fudge that.

Striking green emerald eyes and a kind smile flashed in my mind for a fleeting moment. Gripped my coffee mug a little tight.

"Seriously mate, you want me to book you guys a hotel room?" Billby didn't jest.

Guess I could see if there's any overtime available at work. That passes the time and I get paid for it. Who knows, might actually learn something.

"Not likely, mate."

Huh? What's all the noise from the hallway?

Sounded like... boxes? Heavy things being dragged and plonked? Voices?

I place my ear gently against my front door, cold wood pressing against me, carefully trying to hear. Can't make out much more than that.

"I mean, you could just open the door, mate?" Billby didn't gently suggest.

The flat next to mine had been empty for months now. Quiet. Peaceful. My nice little buffer from the rest of the building. Was that about to change?

"New stranger. New danger."

Hand shook, placing it on the knob. Whatever was happening was probably nothing to do with me anyway, right? I mean, nothing around here ever was. Made a point of avoiding people here.

"Stay alone. Stay safe. Stay alive."

Hand shook harder, gripping the knob. Couldn't see anything from my peephole—angle was wrong, just showed the staircase going up. But I could still hear them. Scraping. Grunting. Someone laughing.

"Step away from the door!" Billby didn't roar.

Hand turned the knob. Opened it, heart skipping a beat, breathing shallow, pulse in my ears—

Quickly slammed the door shut, slumped against it. One, two, in, out.

"Coward."

Frowned, glaring at my lifeless teddy bear's face. Wonder what he'd say right now if he could talk? Would he judge me?

"Never."

He probably would. Probably in a sarcastic way that I'd never be able to tell. Never was good with that, gullible little numpty me. My older brother loved taking advantage of that. That is, until he—why—how could—

"Calm. Focus."

I've got it! Leftover pizza! I didn't mind it cold, really. Still tasted perfectly alright from the fridge the day after. Maybe even better like this without my peppers or tuna.

Mid bite, echo from a knock on my door and pizza now on the floor. Fudge.

"Carpet hungry, mate?"

Knock again. Chest tight, breath shallow, walls closing—

"Hi! Anyone in there?"

That's... not a voice I recognise. Not even a little. Who on earth was that?

"Guess you could try opening the door, mate? Not bloody rocket science, is it," Billby didn't mock.

Hand shook, turned the knob, deep breath and—wow.

"Hi! I'm Sophie. Your new neighbor! Moved into the ground floor flat next to yours. Um, just thought it might be nice to introduce ourselves, you know?"

"Ohh, Umm, I'm a—I'm a shellfish," I mumbled.

Oh fudge.

Sophie giggled. "Well, you look human to me. What's your name?" Her eyes drifted past me into my flat. "Oh! Did you drop something? That pizza on your carpet?"

Fudge. The pizza. The bloody pizza still on my carpet behind me, like a murder victim splattered all over my floor.

"Oh! Yes! Pizza! I dropped it, on the carpet, when you knocked, because I was startled, not that you're startling, you're cute—I mean, the knock was—"

"It's alright," Sophie said warmly. "Sorry for scaring you! I'm Sophie, by the way. Did I mention that already?"

"Prawn!" I blurted loudly.

Fudge! Settle down.

"Oh! That's why you're a shellfish, then? I'm sure there's a story behind that. Well, anyway, come to mine for a cup of coffee sometime. Let's get to know each other?"

Staring at me with those bright green emerald eyes. Striking, distinctive, beautiful—

"Uh, you alright Prawn? You look lost almost."

"Oh! Fine, I'm fine. I'm, tea. Tea I like, I like tea."

Sophie giggled. "Yep, got that too. Alrighty, I'm knackered after moving, so I'm laying down. See you soon I hope!"

Finally, she left, heart still hammering in my ears. Took a deep breath once my door was safely closed and bolted once more.

"Carpet's still hungry, mate." Billby didn't mock.

Picked up the pizza slice, now decorated with carpet fibers. Fudge. Bin time then.

"Real smooth, Mr Shellfish. You're never popping your cherry."

"Shut up!" I yell at my inanimate, definitely not talking teddy bear.

"Bloody hell, mate. See the pair on her?"

Heat rising in my cheeks. Not thinking about that. Not thinking about her. Not thinking about—

"The eyes. Same as his. How? Why?"

Now that was an interesting thought. I'd recognise those eyes anywhere—I got lost in them once before, when the pizza guy came in—

"Invaded."

Invaded my flat. They're... the same eyes? That's ridiculous, though. People don't share eyes, so they must just be very similar. Or related even?

"Conspiracy. Take care, be safe."

Nothing to dwell on, I'm sure. Just eyes. Just beautiful, big, green emerald eyes.

"Not the only pair of big—"

"Billby!" I snapped at my lifeless bear. Think I need a cup of tea, my hands still shaking a little.

"Go for that coffee, mate. Lay down, coffee, you do the maths."

Watched the kettle boil. One hundred fifty-two seconds. Tea ready, nice, calming sip. Damn, almost out of milk now though. I was sure I bought enough, I always do?

"Substitute."

Ah bugger, of course. They swapped my four pint for a two pint in my shopping delivery for some sodding reason. Fudge. Guess I'll have to drink black tea next week. Or maybe plot an excursion to the corner shop?

"Dangerous. Stay home, stay safe."

Wasn't far, really. Ten minute walk at most. But maybe I'll do it tomorrow. Fine for now, and besides, I could always ask Sophie for milk. I'm sure she'd help.

"You could ask for it straight from her huge pair of—"

Shook Billby out of my head. Bloody rude bear. He isn't talking, and I'm not him and he's not me. Just a bear, just feeling shook up from yesterday. Two horrible performance reviews, a demotion, and a pizza order that genuinely couldn't have gone any worse.

"Dunno mate. You could have ordered pineapple."

Had to chuckle. That was a good point. Right, well, Saturday is still young and I'm truly bored senseless. Screw it, maybe I'll log in, go see the guild. Why not? I can still be useful, still have fun, don't need to be an officer.

"Demoted. Deflated. Defeated."

Fudge.

Chapter 4 - Magic

I barely remember the rest of my Saturday. But I probably went to bed early, given it's only seven in the morning and I'm already awake. Nice and warm in here, wrapped in my little cocoon.

"Warm. Safe."

Think I left my bear on the gaming desk. Not like me, pretty much take him everywhere. Guess I'd better drag myself out of bed and find a shirt.

Really fancy some cornflakes, but barely enough milk for a cup of tea.

"Ask her."

I guess I could just venture out into the... hallway. Yeah. Go see Sophie, ask for her milk.

"Straight from those—"

I shook my head, popped open the fridge. Cool air gentle against my face, bright light harsh in my eyes. Can't go wrong with a can of pop.

"Get me one, mate," Billby didn't say.

Silly bear. You can't drink fizzy pop.

"Carpets can't eat pizza either, mate."

I sighed as I placed my shaking hand on the handle. Should check the peephole first, make sure I'm ready to head out there.

"Maybe put some trousers on?"

Oh. Right.

A pair of shorts later, I'm back at the door, ready for the hallway once more. Hand on the knob, grip it extra tight until my knuckles turn white, and open it onto the hallway. It seems to stretch on forever in both directions, getting darker and darker the further it goes, twisting, laughing, mocking—

"Shut the door!"

I pulled the door shut and slumped against it, almost tripping over my feet. I could hear Sophie giggling from next door. Fudge. Must have seen that.

"Smooth as sandpaper, mate."

I clasp my head in my hands. Why can't I just be a paladin? Brilliant, gleaming golden armour and holy magic to dispel the darkness around me.

"Wonder what you would be, Billby?" I ask my inanimate teddy bear.

Not sure why I expected anything other than silence. Just a bear, after all.

"Wizard, obviously. I'm pure magic, mate."

I smiled at my teddy bear, imagining him with a little red robe and one of those ridiculous blue wizard hats, flopping down over his back. Bet he'd have a magic wand, too.

"Go see Sophie. Show her yours."

"Billby!" I yelled at my bear, staring at me with a cruel grin on his face. No. No grin, just that same hollow stare I'm used to.

I sigh, staring at the door once more, back on my feet. I don't get it. There are days where these walls feel like an endless expanse, a whole universe in my flat, my mind the limit, my imagination my guide.

"Try magic mushrooms, mate. It'll feel like a universe."

I'm going to pretend my lifeless teddy bear didn't just recommend hallucinogens to me and go see Sophie. She'll quite happily lend me milk, I'm sure, and I can just order more and get it back to her. Everyone wins.

"Go on then. I'll be waiting."

Deep breath, step out into the hallway. Nice and quiet morning, no postie yet, no noise or fuss. Well, for the moment, I'm sure the Ahmeds' baby will start whinging soon.

"Hurry up, mate," Billby didn't suggest.

Right, I'm off to Sophie's door now. *Aww,* she's got a cute little sticker on the front. Looks like a little panda taking a nap. Wonder if that means she's still sleeping?

Can't be, she was giggling. At me. Tripping over myself like a bumbling twit in the hallway.

I sigh, hand hovering over her door. Nah. I'm not gonna bother. Think I'll just go home and have my cereal with water. Can't be that bad, right?

"Oh hi, Prawn!" Sophie cheerfully announces, her door flying open. Bloody hell, heart stopped beating for a second there.

"Sorry, didn't mean to startle you. You coming to see me?"

How'd she know I was there? Unlucky timing, I guess.

"Oh, um, Sophie, hi, Sophie. Um, can I drink your milk, please?"

Oh fudge. FUDGE. Fudgityfudgingtonfudgeyfudge—

"Buy a girl dinner first, Prawn! But not shellfish, I'm allergic. Oh dear, does that mean we can't be friends?"

Something about her smile and those eerily familiar emerald eyes just made me want to smile back. Felt my mouth complying as though it were ordered.

"Uh, sorry. Can I borrow your milk?"

"Borrow? Well, I don't want it back when it comes out again, Prawn, so no, you can have it!"

Felt myself chuckling a little. Then my chest heaving as I properly laughed. Then my smile faded in a flash, Sophie giggling through the wall popping back into my head. Fudge.

She handed me milk, half empty. Enough to last until groceries. Awesome.

"Uh, kind of you. You're kind, I mean. Either works really," I mumbled.

"No problem! Hey, take my number down. Drop me a message?"

I frowned at the thought of that. Fudge. Too unsafe, too personal, too... settle down and think, Prawn.

"Um, left my phone. At home, I mean. Phone at home."

Sophie gestured towards my front door. "You mean your home right there, next door to mine?"

Cheshire cat grin on her face, twinkle in her annoyingly enthralling emerald eyes. Just couldn't stop staring at them, every bit as unique and beautiful as his. How did she have his eyes?

"Oh, I'm, oh, right. Of course."

Sophie giggled, leaned against her doorway as I shuffled back to my flat. I grabbed my phone from the side, fumbled it into my pocket. Shoved the milk into the fridge and hurried back to the door.

"The eyes," Billby didn't warn.

"There you are, Prawn," Sophie said, now stood at my door, phone at the ready.

It's fine. I can take her number, and not text, so she doesn't get mine. Nice and simple, nice and safe.

"Here, hand me your phone?" Sophie asked, smile on her face, smile in her eyes.

Fudge. Settle down, just a number from a neighbour. Don't have to share mine or use it, unless there's a neighbourly need.

"There we go! I'm in your contacts now. Let me just dial myself so I get yours."

Fudge! Fudge fudge fudge! Billby, help!

24

"Grab it back!"

I reach out and snatch my phone back, startling Sophie. It was too late, as I heard a ringtone jingling away on her phone. I recognised it, but I'm not sure from where.

"Gosh! Manners, Prawn. You feeling alright?"

Settle down. Settle down. Deep breath.

"Fine, I'm. I'm fine, thanks, sorry, didn't mean to snatch!"

Sophie giggled. "Nothing wrong with a bit of enthusiasm. Well, I'm heading out soon, show people some houses I'll never be able to afford. Not even *remotely* jealous. Bye, Prawn!"

I close my door, slump against it, carpet against my backside.

"Could have been worse," Billby didn't gently suggest.

Not bloody sure how. Ugh. She had my number now. Hopefully she wouldn't need to use it, maybe just for certain emergen—

*"Hi Prawn! Saved you as the Prawn emoji. lol.
Soph xx"*

Fudge.

No idea what I'm meant to do now. Hmm. I could forget to save the number, accidentally on purpose? Or just not reply? I stared at the text like I was reading a novel, phone screen glaring at my eyes. It buzzed again, her sending another—just the prawn emoji this time.

"Keen. Too keen?"

Hmm. She did seem overly friendly for someone who met me yesterday, didn't she? Or maybe she was just nice, just normal, just looking to connect to someone in her new home?

"The eyes."

But she did have secrets, I could see that. I just couldn't stop imagining those striking, emerald green eyes, gazing right into my soul. Little things never bother me, so why did they?

"You serious, mate?" Billby didn't mock.

It's fine. I'll just save her as Sophie, uh... I didn't think to ask her surname. Guess I'll just use the panda emoji— is there a panda emoji? There's a panda on her door, so I guess it makes sense. Maybe I can—

"Settle down, mate. Christ."

There we go. Really don't want to reply though, it creates obligation. She'll text back, then I'll have to, then she'll have to, then—

"Already bored, mate. Go game."

Great, I'll just respond with the panda face emoji. That'll do. She'll likely not bother to respond after that. Not exactly much of an obligation, is it?

There we go, that's sent, phone can go off now. Out of sight, out of—

Buzz.

"Aww! Like my sticker! You noticed. We can be a team, Panda and Prawn! xx"

Fudge.

"Ignore it. Game."

I wanted to go be Prawnstar, smiting the foes of our guild. But they shunned me, pushed me aside, replaced—

"Grow up. Play."

I shook my head, sat at my computer. Phone buzzed again.

"Coffee in the communal room later? Soph xx"

Fudge, not dealing with that. Headset on, earmuffs cool and soft against my skin. I click onto the guild voice chat, seeing Badger and Violet on.

"Prawnstar! Mate, you're here!" Badger exclaimed.

"Hey, mate. Yeah, I'm back. Let's go dungeon diving?"

"Absolutely. Violet, you in?"

"Prawn, that you? Haven't seen you in ages! Yep, let's go, boys." Violet cheerily announced.

This was safe. This was happy. There I was, golden armour, gleaming in the guild hall, surrounded by the stone castle walls, forest surrounding us. Violet on her deadly little rogue, and Badger with his cleric. Just some friends having fun, no officers, no performance reviews, no teams or communal room coffees.

Phone buzzed again. Face down on the desk, turned off. Not looking at that. Prawnstar, back in action, reporting for duty!

"Shunned. Ousted."

Fudge.

Chapter 5 - TUNA

"Sorry, guys, think I've had enough gaming for the day. Already worn out."

"Good to have you back, Prawn. Don't be a stranger?" Badger said.

"He couldn't possibly get any stranger," Violet jabbed.

"Easy for you to say, Violet. Think you wrote the book on being a weirdo."

"Oh! Prawnstar with the snap back! Get told, Violet!" Badger roared.

"Later, nerds," I said, cancelling the call, headset off and plonked on the desk once more.

"Shunned."

I didn't need to be an officer to be a part of the guild. I was happy just belonging, having friends, being great at what I do.

"Yeah and I'm the Easter bunny, mate," Billby didn't mock.

"Ugh. Whose side are you on, bloody bear?"

Silence. Just stared at me, hollow, unchanging face as ever.

I sighed, looking at the electric brick turned upside down on my desk. My hand shook as I gripped it. Didn't want to turn it back on, really, but felt I had to.

Screen glared at me as it woke to life. I'd no idea how people stared at these things for so long without getting dizzy.

"Mate, you just gamed for six hours."
More fudging texts.

*"Hey, kiddo. I'm up your way in a few weeks.
Still don't have your address—you avoiding
your old man?"*

A frown formed fast, staring at the screen as it stared right back.
"Bad son."
Accused me of negligence. Bit rich, coming from him. Tim's lifeless eyes, the walls closing, screaming, crying, CRYING SCREAMING SCRATCHING—
"Settle down."
I took a few deep breaths, collapsed onto my sofa. Closed my eyes. Held Billby tight against my chest, bubble, shield, pillow.
"I'm here."
Right. Settle down, more texts. Sophie again?

*"I'll drag you outta there myself if I have to,
Prawn! Come on, coffee time! xx"*

Fudge. Could she actually do that? I mean, she looked kinda strong for a girl, but I had three locks on my door and—
"Hypnosis. Eyes."
Fudge. I really should text Dad back. I haven't in some time, truth be told. He's sent me six texts I haven't answered now.
"Later. Sophie."
Right. Focus on the problem at hand. I really don't want to go to the communal room! Besides... why there? Were the others going?
"Great. Crowds. Fun."
Anything but. Can't stand people, especially more than one at a time. Fudge.

Knot in my stomach. Was I really that anxious about going?

"*Hungry.*"

Oh fudge! I hadn't even had lunch yet. It was, uh, six? Bloody hell, where'd the time go!

"*Dungeons.*"

Right. Well, no pizza left. That would be nice and easy, wouldn't it.

"*Call them again. Hilarious.*"

Never gonna happen. But I really couldn't be bothered to cook, and ugh, that half-price phone deal.

"*Prepare.*"

That's a great idea! I'll write a script. It'll go so much easier this time. Right, I want tuna and pepper, and I want the half-price offer. My name is Prawn. I can do this! I'll get a large and save some.

"*Share.*"

Bears don't need pizza.

"*Sophie does. Shove a slice right in that mouth and—*"

I shook my head. Hand shook too. Phone to ear, gripped tight. Dialling, echoing through my skull.

"Spicy Pizza Palace, order please?"

"Hello, um, I'm ordering a pizza."

"No shit, Sherlock?"

Fudge. That was—that was—mean, you git!

"Um. Yes, pizza. I'm Prawn."

"We don't sell bloody prawn pizzas, mate. Now what'll ya have?"

"Cheese."

Not bloody again! Fudge!

"Right, cheese, and—"

"Fudge!"

"Sir, we don't bloody do fudge on pizza! You some kind of weirdo? Bloody hell. So cheese, what size?"

"TUNA!"

"Bloody hell, calm down there, will ya. Right, cheese, tuna. Great. Anything—"

"Peppers! Pepper pepper tuna cheese—"

"Jesus! Lay off the bloody wacky backy, will ya. Christ. Now what size already?"

"Um, tuna?"

"There a bloody gas leak in this bloody village? Bloody hell. Sending you a medium. Twenty quid, half hour. They don't pay me enough for this bullsh—"

Click.

Well... that went well. Yeah, it did. Yeah! I'm happy with that. Perfectly fine.

"Half price. Large."

Oh fudge it. Well, at least there will be peppers and tuna this time, so that's something.

"Small victories."

Yeah. Huh? Knock on my door? That was quick—

"Prawn? You there! It's Panda!"

Oh. Fudge.

"Get up. Answer," Billby didn't command.

Guess I should just tell her I'm busy. Oh wait, perfect! I'm waiting for a pizza! I can send her away.

I hop to my feet, hand on doorknob. Pull it open, heart skipping a beat as I stare into those emerald eyes, her smile reaching them.

"Hi, Prawn! You coming?"

"Um, hi Pan—Sophie. I'm, I've got pizza, soon, coming soon. Half hour."

"Oh! Where'd you order from?"

"Oh, err, Palace. Spicy Pizza Palace."

Her eyes lit up. "No way! My brother works there! He might even deliver it!"

"Um, well, that's cool, that's, uh, I can't go to the room. Your room, I mean."

"Communal room?"

"Right. Pizza. Pizza coming."

Sophie giggled and gestured to the communal room across the hallway. Oh. Right. Literally opposite my flat.

"Don't think you'll miss him. Come on, then."

Fudge it. How can I get out of this? Was I trapped? Billby, *help?*

Silence. Bloody bear!

"Come on, Prawn." Sophie held out her hand, gentle smile on her face. Oh... fudge.

OK. I can do this. Just a hand, just a communal room, just a pizza. Easy. Her hand felt incredibly soft in mine, skin warm to the touch. The communal room hadn't changed since I last saw it, still bigger than any of our flats. Lease agreement made the landlords keep it—certain they'd rather just chop it up into two more flats and rent them both out for more income, if they could.

Chairs sat round a large table, a sink, kettle and small fridge nearby. Plants in the corner, a sofa against the wall, and pictures of various residents and their group activities from over the years adorned the walls. Sophie went and sat down on the sofa as I hovered in the doorway.

"Um, what am I doing here?" I cautiously ask.

"Come sit, Prawn? Meeting happening here in a few minutes, I'm told. Aren't you in the building group chat?"

"Oh, uh, no. Never joined."

Sophie smiled warmly. "Hop in it tonight then, silly! You can stay up to date with the households."

Oh fudge. Can't think of anything worse. I found myself missing my teddy bear, even though he was only a few metres away, back in my sanctuary.

"Sophie, lovely to see you!" Karen said, brushing past me to enter the room.

"Oh!" She turned and stared at me like she'd seen a ghost. "Bloody hell, sorry, Peter. I swear I somehow didn't see you! Chameleon, aren't you?"

She walked right past me! What the fudge is she on about? I'm... how couldn't she—not exactly bloody invisible, am I?

"Peter?"

"Oh! I'm, um, sorry, Karen. Nice to see you."

"Yeah. Haven't seen you in some time. You keeping well?"

"Work. Hard. Working, hard." I mumble.

"That's lovely. Well, good to see you participating. You were missed."

What did that mean? Was that a jab, hidden as a compliment? Kindness obscuring malice? Her smile hid from her eyes, her lies hid from her truth. Never did trust Karen. Fudge it, miss my bear.

Loud knock from my front door? Oh! The pizza!

"Um, gotta go. Got pizza, nice to see the, um, see you!"

"Wait, Prawn, I—" Sophie started, but I was already gone like the wind. Dashed outta there like my stomach depended on it. If it was important, she could text it anyway, I guess. No big deal.

"Oh, hi, mate! Prawn, weren't it?" Marcus said, big smile, pizza in his hand.

Oh FUDGE! I don't have a tip for him again! Just another twenty! Wait, hold on, the box is the wrong size?

"Check it out, mate. I got them to make you a large, no extra cost. Since you were so cool to me Friday."

Aw, that was... that... that was sweet. Kind. Heartwarming, even. Felt myself grin, wide. What a sweet man. Sweet man with striking, emerald green eyes that pierced my soul, just like Sophie.

"Oh! So kind! Kind of you, so kind. Um, thanks. Want a slice?"

Marcus laughed. "Thought you'd never ask, mate. In your flat again?"

Oh god. Fudge no. No fudging way. Think, Prawn!

"Oh, uh, the communal. Um, over here, come with, ma—mate."

"Sure, sure."

Marcus followed after me, cap worn, head low, pizza in his hand. Could smell the tuna and the peppers. Maybe Sophie and Karen would want a piece too, which was bad, but at least I kept him out of my flat.

"Marcus! How you doing, bro?" Sophie said, rushing up from the sofa to give him a hug.

Well fudge! Siblings! Those eyes. No conspiracy, just genetics. Adorable.

"Hey, Panda pop. Just delivering a pizza to this legend here," Marcus started, gesturing to me. "You know he let me have a slice of his last one? Doesn't know me from Adam. What a cool guy."

Me? Cool? Yeah! Me! Yeah, I'm cool! Real cool! Cool like a block of ice sat atop Mount Everest!

"Pizza!" I announced cheerily.

"You sharing?" Karen asked, grin forming.

Fudge. I wanted the leftovers for tomorrow. Oh fudge it, let's do this. Can't be shellfish.

"Yep. Yep, sure am. Enjoy."

We sat and shared pizza together, the four of us. We were soon joined by Ali from upstairs and Denise too.

"Communal room hasn't been this busy in a while," Denise muttered, smile on her face. Her hair was greying, but her brown eyes still full of life for a woman in her early fifties.

"So good to see you all. Zara sends her love. You too, Mr Awning. Not used to seeing you so often."

Ali was all business. Or was he? He did seem fatherly, warm, in his own way. Did have a baby, I guess, though I didn't get the whole praying thing. Still, his burden, not mine.

"Um, lovely to see everyone. I um, I'll go now."

Phew. Chest felt tight, pulse fast in my ears. Think I've had enough of this crowd.

"Hold on, Peter," Karen said as I set a foot outside the door. "You want to join our group chat now?"

Fudge. Just be honest. Just settle down, and be honest.

"Um, group chats are too busy for me. Can't really, I'm sorry, I can't. Busy."

"Oh, Prawn!" Sophie interjected. "You can join and just mute the notifications. Then you can reach out if you need it, but no obligations!" she added helpfully. Very helpfully. Incredibly helpfully. Fudging helpfully.

"I, um, I can't think of a reason why I could say no to that," I mumbled with a frown.

Fudge it. Fudging Sophie and her fudging gorgeous damn eyes. Oh, when had Marcus left? Guess a while ago. Pizzas to deliver, no doubt.

"Great! We'll pop you in. See you soon!"

I smiled like a wounded doe and limped my way back to my flat. Closed door, all three locks secured, deadbolt and all.

"Exposed."

Fudge. I was. They would soon add me to the damn building chat. Ugh. Could already hear the relentless buzzing.

"Siblings."

Yeah. Marcus and Sophie had the same eyes because they were related. Sweet, I think.

"Same building. Related. Coincidences?"

Fudge.

Chapter 6 - Coward

"Look, sir. I appreciate that you feel it's fraud, but let's go over the facts. You still have your card, right?"

"Yeah?"

"And they knew your PIN number?"

"Must have guessed it. Got lucky."

Couldn't help but grin. Some fraudsters were bloody smart. Others, well, others were this guy.

"Sir, they got it right first time, and there's less than a one in six thousand chance of that. Couple that with you still having your card, well—it was either your flatmate who withdrew the three hundred pounds, or Santa Claus. My money isn't on the jolly red fat man, sir."

"You have millions! Can't your bank just give me the money? Ridiculous way to treat a loyal customer."

Entitlement, first party fraud, potato tomato.

"Sorry, sir, this is a civil matter between yourself and your flatmate. May I suggest you contact the Citizens Advice Bu—"

Oh. Already hung up.

"Santa!" Billby didn't chuckle, staring at me from his spot on my work desk.

I did have to chuckle a little. I needed to be careful with the sarcasm, though—if he complained I may be in trouble. I didn't feel I was particularly disrespectful, though? Just trying to convey his ridiculousness with an equally ridiculous measure.

"Cruel. Callous."

Well, thankfully that was my last call of the day. Headset off, Bill and I off to the sofa. Slump onto it, nice and soft, relaxing. Breathe deep, chest tightening as I fumble for my phone in my pocket.

Ugh, more messages.

> *"Missed you yesterday, Prawn! You coming to poetry club? Communal room tonight. Every Thursday from now on if it goes well. Soph xx"*

Hmm. Sounds creative, but not something I've ever tried or considered. Not sure it's for me. Besides—*people.*

"Boring. Just game."

Drag myself to the gaming desk, packet of crisps from the cupboard. That counts as dinner, I'm sure.

"Nutritious."

Bloody bear. Always smile seeing my gaming computer fired up, those beautiful trees in the serene forest on my wallpaper. Looks so peaceful, so tranquil.

"So isolated. So vulnerable."

Hop onto the guild chat, but nobody on. Odd for a Thursday? Well, Badger was online on socials if not the game. Drop him a call.

"Hey, Badger, where's everyone at?"

"Prawnstar! Sup, mate. You didn't hear? We're all playing that new space heist game that came out now."

"But what about the guild, the raids, the—"

"Old news, mate. You buying this or what? We already have a pirate clan, and we just robbed a space station BLIND, mate. You should have seen Violet, she's bloody savage! Spent half the loot on bloody bullets."

Fudge.

"Um, not sure I can justify the expense at this stage, I've bills and—"

"Fuck that noise! I'll buy it for you, mate. You in?"

Fudge! My breathing quickened, chest ached, walls closed—

"Gift. Obligation?" Billby didn't suggest.

"Sorry, Badger," I started, "I'd feel like I owed you, mate, you know?"

Badger laughed out loud. "You forgot who bought me my last two games, clearly. You're taking the backsies, no obligation, just get on and have some fun with us."

Fudge it! Ughhhh. Hmm.

"Um, can't tonight, mate. I've got, uh, I'm poetry club."

Silence.

"You know what, Prawn? My instincts were to laugh at that. Sounds right bloody girly. But maybe it'll be good for you, you know? Get you outta your shell."

Oh. *Nice pun.* Cheeky git.

"Hey! Nice shellfish joke. Bastard!"

Cackled together with Badger for what felt like a long while. Think I needed that.

"Oh, mate, completely by accident, I swear. No really, go do it, mate. Drop us a message later, let us know how it goes. Right, Violet wants me back, next heist awaits. Her trigger finger must be getting antsy. See you soon, bud."

Call ended, and I couldn't help but feel myself smile. Yeah. Think I'd like to give it a go, see what it's all about. I could be a space pirate instead of a paladin. Why not?

"Nerd."

Fudge.

Screw it. What have I got to lose? Slumped on my sofa, fumbled for my phone. Took a deep breath and checked the time, they were meeting in the communal room in less than half an hour.

"Hello, Sophie. I'll be there. Prawn."

Deleted that. Too formal, perhaps? Not formal enough?

"Dear Sophie, I will attend the meeting at your request. Sincerely, Prawn."

Settle down, that's terrible. Stare at my bear, somehow hoping for some inspiration or guidance, but that same hollow stare greets me back. Fine, one more try.

"Yep."

Short, sharp, snappy.

"Crappy," Billby didn't add.

Ugh! I'll just... show up. Yeah. Nothing wrong with that, right? Though—what do I even do? I'm not a poet.

"Investigator."

Ah! I'm not a poet but I can use a search engine. Gather some facts, learn some tips, forge a plan of action. Yeah, that's a great idea!

Twenty minutes of searching later, I heard the rhythmic thudding of stairs as people headed down to the communal room. Did I really want to do this? I still knew next to nothing about poems or prose or—

"Just try."

Right. Just... open my door, give it a go. Head to the communal room, see the others. Well, those who attend, can't imagine everyone will be there. Certainly hope not, anyway—far too many bloody people.

"Coward."

Hand hovering above the knob, pulse quickening. Breaths faster, escalating. Close my eyes door open, hallway taunting and mocking and twisting and—

"Settle down."

Right. Step out into it, drag my wobbly knees over to the communal room. Was this a mistake? Possibly. Probably.

Chapter 7 - Peacock

"Prawn! You're here!" Sophie beamed as I entered the doorway.

Karen, Sophie and Ali sat at the table, all smiling warmly as I approached. My heart pounded in my ears, but their smiles were disarming somehow.

"Good to see you once more, my friend," Ali stated plainly. "All is well?"

"Oh, um, good thank you. I'm well, I mean."

Good worked. No need to second guess myself. Just settle down.

"Take a seat, dear?" Karen suggested, warm grin on her face.

Fudge. Stood there like a lemon. I quickly sat at the opposite end of the table, facing the three of them.

"We don't bite, Prawn! Well, I do eat prawns actually, but I'll make an exception for you!" Sophie patted the chair next to her.

Hold on—didn't she say she was allergic to shellfish? Had I misheard or misunderstood that in some way?

Fudge. I was comfortable over here. The clock was getting pretty loud though. Tick tock. Guess I better had, don't want to be rude.

I shuffled out of my chair and plonked myself next to Sophie. Her green eyes were warm, inviting.

"James, you're here! Is Denise coming?" Karen said, seeing him enter.

"Err, she will be. Probably soon. Just showering." He mumbled meekly, taking my former spot at the end of the table.

Usurper. Interloper. Why couldn't I sit there?

Settle down, Prawn. Just a spot. Not a castle or a kingdom or a guild officer position for a dead guild that's off raiding space stations instead.

Clenched my fists, glaring at the table. I'd spent so long on Prawnstar the paladin. Eight thousand hours down the pan. Fudge.

"So glad you all came!" Karen cheerfully announced.

I hadn't noticed Denise sat next to me! Nearly jumped out of my chair when I spotted her.

"You alright, young man?" she asked cautiously.

"Um, I'm fine thanks. Just startled me. Didn't see you arrive," I admitted honestly.

"Off with the bears again, you," Denise said warmly.

Isn't it supposed to be fairies? What a peculiar thing to say.

"I brought a poem to discuss today," Karen announced. "There's no pressure for anyone to bring or write their own, but no judgment if you do. Safe space. Agreed?"

Safe. I liked the sound of that.

"Um, safe. Agreed, I mean," I mumbled.

Smiles and nods all around as Karen fumbled in her bag for the poem. She cleared her throat and read aloud:

Minds unbound by fear and doubt,

Can stretch beyond the sky to see.

Each new idea, seeds within,

Growing into a greater me.

"Profound," Ali stated simply. "I am often humbled by that which I do not know."

"That was, err, sweet," James stammered.

Denise dabbed at her eyes. "Touching. Moving."

Sophie clapped her hands. "Where did you find that, Karen? I like how it opens your mind to new ideas!"

Karen chuckled and raised her hands. "You got me. I googled it!"

Gentle laughter rippled around the table. I found myself grinning too. She was honest, at least. The poem was... profound? Purposeful? Perfunctory? Some kind of P-word.

"Any thoughts, Prawn?" Sophie asked, smiling gently.

"Peacock," I offered.

Oh fudge.

What the fudge was that? Karen was staring at me. Oh fudge, oh—

"Oh I get it! That's very insightful and sweet, Prawn," Sophie said, smiling gently at me.

"Yeah. I did feel a bit like a peacock unfurling his feathers sharing that. Thanks, Peter," Karen kindly agreed. "Anyone else got something to share?"

Fudge, that was lucky. Lucky or they were being overly kind.

Before I knew it, half an hour had passed. I'd probably rather have been hanging out with Badger, but this honestly wasn't bad. Got me thinking. Feeling, even. Didn't realize poems could do that. Still dreaded the idea of having to bring my own though.

"Honestly," Karen said after some time, "I had a lot of fun with this. Are we thinking weekly?"

Glances and grins exchanged around the room. I forced a smile whenever eyes met mine.

"That seems like a yes!" Sophie announced happily. "Same time next week?"

"Wait!" Denise erupted, jumping up. "Stay right here."

She rushed upstairs. Brief thudding, then back down carrying a bag. My eyes narrowed as she pulled out a series of red shirts with black writing on the front.

"'Bear the Word'?" Ali asked, examining one. "What's this?"

"For our little group!" Denise beamed. "I work at a textile factory—easy to get. Got all sizes! The moment Karen mentioned this, well, I just *had* to!"

The shirts were handed out. Everyone slipped them on. Everyone but me.

"Peter?" Denise held one out expectantly.

Fudge. This felt weird. Off, somehow. But I couldn't draw attention to myself. I took it, pulled it over my head.

"Must confess, bit cult-like isn't it?" James stammered. "The r-red and all."

Nervous laughter from everyone, but I felt a little... I don't know. Something was giving me pause, here.

"Plus 'Bear the Word'!" Karen added, grinning. "Spooky!"

More laughter. I joined in, though I didn't know why. Why could I hear my pulse? Settle down.

Denise frowned slightly. "Sorry. I thought it was clever. I was inspired by Peter, actually."

The laughter stopped.

"That makes sense," Ali said quietly.

Everyone turned to look at me.

All eyes. On me. Staring. Waiting.

"Um, me?" I managed. "Why?"

"Your bear, silly," Sophie said gently. "The one you carry everywhere."

Carry everywhere?

No, I—

I looked down.

Billby.

In my hand.

Right there.

Had been there.

This whole time.

When had I—

I hadn't—

Had I?

"Prawn? You alright?" Sophie's voice sounded distant, like she spoke from the endless flat hallway as it stretched off into oblivion.

I stared at Billby's eyes. Lifeless. Still.

But he'd been there. In my hand. In the communal room. At the table. This whole meeting.

I hadn't noticed.

How had I not noticed?

"He's always with you," Denise said warmly. "It's sweet."

Always.

With me.

Always.

The room tilted sideways. The walls grew darker, closing in. Breathing, fast, rapid, shallow. They were laughing at me. All of them. All pointing, all laughing. Why was everything spinning? Rooms don't spin.

Tired. So tired.

"Prawn? Can you hear me?"

"Sophie? Ugh... what happened?"

I was on the floor. The communal room was nearly empty now—just Sophie crouched beside me and a paramedic checking my pulse.

Not a green goblin. Settle down, Prawn.

"You passed out," Sophie said quietly. "We called an ambulance."

Passed out. Right. I—

"Bit bloody awkward, mate."

That—that voice. No. Can't be.

Not a thought, not a feeling. A voice, as clear as crystal, as real as Sophie. Can't be.

"Oh but it can," Billby did continue. "Nice first poetry club, mate. Smooth as sandpaper. By the way, you just joined a cult. When's the first ritual sacrifice?"

Looked down. Billby in my lap, staring at me. How'd he get there? I was—I was passed out?

Paramedic buggered off once he was satisfied I wasn't dying, but mumbled something about resting and stress and visiting my GP. No thanks.

"How long have I been carrying you?" I tentatively asked Billby.

"Think," Billby didn't say.

I couldn't. I—oh no.

"That's right, mate," Billby began. "Never leave you. Ever. I'm even with you when you're taking a shit, mate."

Fudge.

"Prawn?" Sophie asked, leaning over me, hand gently on my shoulder. "Who are you talking to?"

I met her striking emerald eyes, opened my mouth briefly then closed it again. I couldn't tell her. I couldn't tell anyone.

"Nobody," I mumbled. "Um, thinking. Thinking out loud, I mean."

"LIAR!" Billby roared like a lion, sound hammering my ears. "But I sympathise. Can't tell her about me, can you? They'd section you faster than you can say 'poetry club cult,' mate."

Sophie helped me to my feet, still in her 'Bear the Word' shirt. Found myself staring at the letters as they stared right back at me.

"You're not staring at the words, mate," Billby didn't gently suggest.

Cheeks turned red as cherry as I smiled meekly at Sophie. The twinkle from her emerald eyes was gone, concern painted across them instead.

"Let's get you home, Prawn."

I didn't argue. I appreciated the care, her arm round my shoulder as she walked me to my door. With Billby suddenly heavy in my left hand, gripping him extra tight, fully aware he was there. Would it stay that way?

"Nah mate, you'll forget. Always do. Half bear, half ninja, me," Billby jested.

OK. Did have to smile at that.

At my door, Sophie watched me head inside, then spoke before I closed it.

"Sure you're OK, Prawn? That was scary!"

"Oh, um, I'm yep. Yep, I'm fine. Thanks, Sophie."

Sophie smiled gently. "Don't be embarrassed about your teddy bear, Prawn. I've got one myself called Mr Panda, oh and Mr Cheesecake too! Both so soft and cuddly, when it gets lonely at night, you know? Sleep with them both every night!"

Felt myself smiling back at Sophie. It reached my eyes. Plonked Billby on the side and stepped back out into the hallway again.

"Um, thanks, thank you. You're kind. Hug?"

FUDGE! Why'd I say that! What the fudge! Oh—

Her arms around me, her body warm, soft. Her hug didn't put the broken pieces back together, but it came bloody close. I hugged her back tight for just a moment, before pulling away.

"Um uh, thanks. Thank you. For you know, everything."

"That's what friends are for. Bye!"

Took a few steps back to her own flat, disappearing inside. Back in mine, deadbolt secured, slumped against the door.

47

"Right then, Casanova," Billby began, somehow back in my hand. "Think we better have ourselves a little chat, hadn't we?"

Chapter 8 - Just

Sat myself down on the sofa. My sanctuary, my fortress, my—

"Prison," Billby didn't interrupt.

"That's not fair," I muttered. "I go on quests all the time. Just last week, I led a raid into—"

"Mate, I'm already bored—shut up about your game already. I'm more interested in the game you don't realise you're playing," Billby said ominously.

What the hell did that mean? Something felt... different. Somehow I could hear him as though he were talking, and yet—

"Exposition is bloody boring, mate. Get over it. You can hear me, so what. Am I a hallucination? There a gas leak in the building? Possessed by a demon? A deity? Who gives a flying fudge. You can hear me, and I'm here to help."

That was the longest, most verbose... thought? Speech? I'm not even sure anymore—I'd ever heard or imagined from Billby.

"Bored. So, you joined a cult, by the way. Nice going there. When's the first ritual sacrifice? Think it'll be you?"

"Not funny," I mutter meekly back to my bear. My lifeless stuffed bear, clutched against my chest like a beacon in the darkness, like a shield from the fear.

"More like from the cult, mate," Billby didn't mock. "Bear the bloody Word? Might as well say 'Cult of the

bloody bear' mate. Think they have good pension plans in a cult?"

"No, you're—"

"Wrong? Go ahead. Search it. I'll wait."

"You're being—"

"Ridiculous? Matching shirts. Poems about expanding your minds and growing. Yeah, not cult-like at all, is it, mate. S'pose they could just be humouring you, after all, you're known as a relaxed and funny guy."

Did he actually have a point? He was being ridiculous.

"Sophie—overly nice. She's not into you, mate. Girl like that could pull a bloke a day if she fancied it. So why so bloody nice? And don't even get me started on that peacock bit."

"Um, what peacock bit?"

"You proper miffed it, mate. Nailed it with a rubber hammer, if you get me. Yet they loved it anyway? Give me a break, mate. Love-bombing your gullible shellfish arse."

Right, enough of this bullfudge. I'm going to search online for 'Bear the Word' to shut this bear up. I will. I'll do it.

"Get on with it then. Snore," Billby didn't goad.

Sat at my desk, fingers trembling as my hands hovered over the keys. Paused a beat and closed my eyes before hitting enter.

Word Bearers? Oh Billby, you silly sausage. Just a fictional group from a game. Nothing special or—

"Keep digging. First result and you've had enough? I could search better and I've got furry paws. Open your eyes, mate."

Fine, fine. Hold on, what's this? The Cult of the Bear and those who 'Bear the Word'?

That's... terrifying, actually. Red robes, all holding teddy bears in their pictures. They... I can't look at this. I need out of this.

"You MUST look. You need to see what you're up against. I'm not joking, Prawn. I'm here to keep you SAFE. You would look pretty great in a red robe, though. Right up until the ritual dagger in the ribs."

Scratched at my chest. No, this was ridiculous. They were just kind, friendly, nice people and nothing more.

"Check your group chat. Go ahead, I dare you. Been buzzing away in the background whilst you've been buried in a screen. I know where your head would rather be buried, but we'll—"

"Zip it, Billby," I demanded forcefully.

Silence. Good.

Phone buzzed again. Right, settle down, let's have a look.

New group made, Sophie adding me. 'Bear the Word'.

Nothing abnormal about that—they want a group chat for poetry club. Simple, normal, typical.

But... these messages.

Sophie: "Hope you're feeling better, Prawn!"

Karen: "Rest up, see you next week."

Ali: "Peace be with you."

Denise: "So sorry if the shirts startled you!"

Oh rats. Rats, cats, bats.

"Don't you mean fudge?"

"Oh, go pack some of that yourself, Billby," I snapped sharply in reply.

My chest sunk instantly forming a frown. That wasn't kind, or fair. That was just plain—

"Mean. Cruel."

Yeah.

"Look at all that affection, Prawn. Got to keep their newest recruit sweet, don't they?"

"Just being kind," I mumbled.

51

"Look at the timing, the coordination of it. Even you can see it doesn't add up."

Felt that comment jab at my ribs somehow, but not sure why.

Suppose I should reply, settle them down.

"Thank you"

I tapped that out in reply. That would do, right? Nice and simple, just the two words. Hit send.

"Mistake," Billby didn't mock.

Right, bloody bear was annoying me now. If there was something wrong with my reply, and he's here to keep me safe, why not let me know before I bloody sent it?

"I ain't your mum, mate. Figure some stuff out for yourself."

Felt a tear trickle down my cheek, felt like sandpaper against my skin. Wiped it away quickly.

Phone buzzed again. Poetry cult once more. Club. Club.

Sophie: "Karen has a theme for next week's poetry club!"

Karen: "Sure do. Eldritch horrors and obscure Deities!"

Um. What?

"TOLD YOU," Billby roared like thunder.

Denise: "Quirky! I'm in."

Ali: "Challenging. I accept."

James: "I'll try."

"Not even a day later, mate, and it's already phase two. Minds unbound to accept their new deity. Can you finally see my point? Do I need to drill it into your skull myself? My furry little paws ain't exactly made for DIY, mate."

Damn it, Billby. It's just a—

"Just a this, just a that. So many atrocities throughout history started with a 'just', Prawn."

I sighed, staring at the red robes still on my monitor. I couldn't argue—that was true. But Billby was wrong here. It was just a fun theme, just—

"There you go with that word again. Just this, just that. Just justifying a cult. Just."

My head ached. So tired. Left my computer and slumped on the sofa once more, staring at the counter. Phone buzzed again.

> Sophie: "Starting a spreadsheet of genres and poems we can use to track what everyone enjoys and doesn't. Good idea?"

> Karen: "Love it. Message Sophie privately, everyone."

Fudge.

Closed my eyes for a while. Just needed some space for a moment, just—

"Just, just, just. Just get up and go back to searching. Knowledge is power, so cults limit it. Do it," Billby commanded.

No way. I was exhausted, and the last thing I was doing was getting up from this comfy sofa.

Or so I thought—now sat at my desk, search engine open once more. Fudge.

'Bearing Witness: Words and Psychological Themes in Cults'

Hand shook, mouse hovering over the link. This was ridiculous. It was just—

"Just."

Took a deep breath, closed my eyes, and clicked the link.

Symbolic identities, matching clothing, shared phrasing, ritualistic meetings—all designed to create a sense of belonging that overrides individual judgement.

"Tell me that's not what you've been seeing. Call me crazy," Billby said plainly.

Opened my mouth to speak the words, but nothing came out. A word I just couldn't bear to call him.

"Didn't think you could. Look, take a bucket of salt with my words if you want, Prawn. But at least consider them?" Billby gently suggested.

This didn't make any sense. Just a block of flats in a little Norfolk village, not some cultist movement. Literally just a poetry club. Nothing more, just that.

"Just, just, justify."

Fudge.

Moments later, phone buzzed with a text.

"Hi Prawn, Sophie. You feeling any better? Want me to come over? I don't know about you, but I could use a hug xx"

"Jesus, Prawn," Billby started. "That's a red robe."

"Don't you mean flag?"

"Potato, tomato. Be bloody careful. She wants into your SANCTUARY. And she wants... a hug? Are you sure it's just that? You've seen the way she looks at you with those hypnotic emerald eyes. Has she had formal training? Be very bloody careful, Prawn."

Shook the worries away. Just a friend, just a hug, just—

"Just."

No! Screw it. She asked for a hug from a friend and she's getting one.

"Don't go out there, Prawn. You're still vulnerable. Stay here, stay safe."

I sighed, slumped back on the sofa. Maybe he was right. But I needed to reply to this, or she might come knock. I didn't want that.

"Scare her away. Ask if hug is code for sex. Do it."

Gripped Billby tight, glaring at him. He was starting to really... frustrate me.

"You're frustrated because you're a bloody virgin, mate," Billby didn't mock.

Focus. Hand on phone, bum on sofa, fingers hovering over buttons.

"Hi Sophie. Flat a bit untidy. Maybe later?"

That would work. Short, sharp, punchy.

"Perfect."

"Great! I'll be right over, help you tidy. Give me five."

Fudge.

"Fudge? Yeah, that don't cut it, mate. You're fucked. Sanctuary? Five minutes and it'll be a post-apocalypse, mate."

FUDGE!

Four minutes. I had four minutes.

Computer—close all tabs. Red shirt, quickly pulled back over my head. Billby—put down somewhere normal, not clutched to my chest like a shield.

I set him on the sofa.

Looked away.

Looked back.

Billby was in my hand again.

"Can't get rid of me that easy, mate. Besides, you'll NEED me when she gets here. Someone's got to watch what she's actually doing while you're distracted by those hypnotic... eyes."

Knock at the door.

Three knocks. Friendly. Normal.

Terrifying.

"Showtime, Prawn," Billby whispered. "Remember: she's here to assess the situation. To see what you know. To report back to the others. Don't. Trust. Her."

My hand shook as I reached for the lock.

"Be brave, Prawn. I'm here."

Chapter 9 - Pear

Deep breath, steady hand, door open.

"Hi Prawn!" Sophie beamed, standing in my doorway like a beacon shining in the darkness surrounding her. She was beaut—

"Settle down," Billby didn't snap.

Right, right. Fudge, last thing I want to be thinking. Not going to let myself have a crush on a cultist.

"You gonna let me in, Prawn, or just keep staring at me?" Sophie joked, giggling.

"Oh, uh, sorry. Um, we could go to the communal room for coffee?" I found myself suggesting.

Felt like Billby approved of that. Got her away from the sanctuary.

"Come on, you. I'm here to help. What needs tidying?"

Fudge. Nothing. Absolutely nothing. If I got any more tidy, my flat might as well be a show home. Ohhhhh fudge.

"Uh, oh I know! Dates. I've got, uh, expiry dates. On tins and things. But it's not a big deal—"

"Nonsense," Sophie said, gently pushing past me. "Oh, and you're wearing your poetry club shirt still! So cute! Do you like my one?"

Oh fudge. How the hell was I supposed to respond to that? It was a tank top with a smiling cheesecake on the front. Right, settle down, and compliment the cheesecake, not the... uh... huge personalities on display.

Ugh, why did it have to be summer. I swear I could hear Billby snickering at me, but I failed to see how this was funny.

"Yep, I love your, um, the pear. Cheesecake."

"Lemon, actually! Isn't he cute?"

He kind of was, actually. Put me at ease, his great big happy smile. Friendly little fella.

"Just look. Your neck will snap," Billby didn't helpfully suggest.

Helpful or cruel, who could say.

"Wow, Prawn, you keep your flat a lot tidier than mine. Let's go through your cupboards, then."

Sophie made herself at home, rootling through my cupboards, checking the dates on things.

"Oops! These soups are expired."

I sighed deep. Glad she found something to chuck, or I might be even more nervous.

If that were even bloody possible.

"Well, that was quick, Prawn! Honestly, you're too anxious. Your place is spotless! Can I sit?"

Fudge! I just want her to go. I'm not safe. I'm not—

"Yep," I meekly mumbled, gesturing to my sofa. What the bloody hell was I fudging doing! I need her to go!

I searched around for Billby, but I couldn't find him anywhere. He would know what to do. Where was he?

"We need to practice your hosting skills, Prawn. Haven't even offered a girl a drink yet!" Sophie snickered.

Fudge, hadn't even considered that! Um, think. Drinks. Does she mean... alcohol? Not my thing. Uh, maybe just tea? No, seems too informal. What about—

"Prawn?"

"Oh! Sorry! Um, I've got, water?"

Water? Water. Really.

Sophie grinned like a Cheshire cat. "Well, I would hope so! Anything more interesting?"

Oh fudge! What could be more interesting than water? This felt like a test I hadn't studied for. Milk, maybe? I'm just going to list. Yeah, I like lists.

"Milk, Pepsi, coffee, tea, Ribena, lemon—"

"I'll take a Pepsi. Thanks, Prawn."

Right, sorted. Hand on fridge, pulled it open a little hard. Hand shook as hers met mine on the cold, wet can.

"Oops! Sorry, Prawn," she smiled as our skin met on the metal.

Ugh. My pulse was in my ears, sweat beading on my brow. Damn it, where was my bear?

"You OK, Prawn?" Sophie gently asked.

"Um, hot. I mean, the summer. Not, I mean, uh. Summer is hot."

Fudge! Settle down, Prawn.

"Hence the tank top! Ditch this too, if it was socially acceptable!"

Oh FUDGE. Why. WHY. I didn't need that image in my head. Oh fudgefudgefudge—

"You two coming to sit down then?" Sophie suggested, smiling.

Two? Oh.

There he was. In my hand, like last time.

"Miss me?" Billby didn't mock. *"You seem to be doing fine without me. Well, maybe not actually."*

Shook my head, joined Sophie at the opposite end of the sofa.

"I don't bite, Prawn! Come cuddle?"

WHAT? WHAT!? No! That's—what in the—

"Just teasing! You're so easy to wind up. We need to find a way to unwind you, Prawn—you're all coiled up like a spring. So what do you do for fun?"

Fun? Fun. Fudge.

"Psst, Prawn mate," Billby didn't whisper. *"Got an idea how she can help you release that tension."*

NOT listening to that. Sodding bear.

Right, fun. Fun, fun, fun.

"Oh! Uh, I work. And I got, the game. I game." I stated.

"Oh! That sounds fun. That your office, over there?"

Sophie stood, approaching the door to my inner sanctum. The room holding my secrets, my shame, my soul.

"Stop her!" Billby roared. "Quick! Start a fire!"

"Stop! Fire!?" I didn't yell. "Can't let anyone in my office. Work, um, confidentiality."

"Oh," Sophie frowned, hand now off the door handle. "That's OK. What games do you play, then?"

Sophie came and joined me on the sofa. Before I knew it, an entire hour had passed. I had no idea she liked the same games as me, and we ended up swapping online handles, despite my trepidation. Hadn't honestly had that much fun in some time.

"Well, was really fun to spend some time with you, Prawn. Drop Sophinator a message!"

"Um, yep! Will do. Th-thanks!"

Closed my door, slumped against it, breathing a deep, long sigh of relief.

"Well," Billby began. "That was a bloody catastrophe, wasn't it?"

Was it? It didn't feel like one. It felt... tense, certainly. My chest was tight just thinking about... hers.

"Exactly my point, mate," Billby said. "Got the bloody watermelons out like a pair of hypnodiscs, programming your mind."

"No! They didn't come out, they—"

"Tank top didn't exactly leave much to the imagination, did it, mate? Cult classic. Lure 'em in to the penis fly trap, mate. You heard her—only reason her top stayed on? Socially acceptable. She tested your resolve. You almost bloody snapped."

That... that wasn't true. She was sweet, kind, friendly, fun—

"All the qualities needed for a great cult recruiter, Prawn. Lure you in, hook you, corrupt you. Potato, tomato."

"You're being paranoid," I snapped.

"Am I? Wouldn't take no for an answer. Pretty much went straight for your office, mate, and we both know what's in there. She can never, ever see it. We both know that."

"I... I know," I mumbled meekly. "I know."

But Billby was being ridiculous. Just a poetry club, just a friendly—

"Just."

Fudge.

"You're not being fair," I said to Billby, tears welling in my eyes. "Not everyone is out to get me. I deserve friends! I deserve a life! I deserve—"

"I deserve, I, I, me, me, me. Bit shellfish, mate. Look, I'm not saying you don't, Prawn. You know I'm here to protect you. But you can't let your loneliness stop you from being a critical thinker. What's the point of getting your end away if they end you?"

That comment dug into my ribs hard. It felt cruel, but it also felt right. Tears welled in my eyes as I pictured Sophie smiling warmly at me from my sofa.

"I know. But I think you're being ridiculous about this whole cult thing, Billby."

"Are you sure? You did the research."

Fudge. Honestly? I wasn't. I wanted to call Billby crazy, but not everything about the situation added up. The shirts were ready on the first night, the poem was about accepting new truths and expanding your mind, and now we're discussing Eldritch horrors?

It could all be coincidence. But it also couldn't, and I needed to go into this with my eyes wide open.

"I'm here, mate. I'll keep you safe, I always do. You don't make it bloody easy for me though mate."

"Thanks, Billby."

Gave my bear a great big hug and settled into the sofa. Sure there'd be something fun on the telly.

Chapter 10 - Knot

"Um, can you hear me?" I mumbled on the voice chat.

"Yep! Loud and clear!" Sophinator said back. "So let's game! Love your name, by the way. Prawnstar. So funny!"

Had to smile at that. It was a dumb online handle I made at thirteen, thinking I was so clever and unique. Guess it just stuck, but my cheeks did turn red at the comment.

"Thanks. Uh, hmm. Let me think what to play."

Badger bought me that new space heist game. Honestly looked like a lot of fun, though I missed the guild and my paladin. But did I really want to introduce Sophie to everyone? What do I even introduce her as? My neighbour? My friend?

"My recruiter," Billby helpfully added.

Thanks, Billby. Fudge.

"Prawn, I'm dying of old age! Pick a game!"

Oh fudge. Fine, let's just play a puzzle game. Nice and easy, nice and simple.

"More important puzzles to be sorting, mate," Billby prodded.

I shook my head, focusing on the screen.

"Uh, let's try, um, you ever played the Portal puzzle games?"

"No! Bought them ages ago, never did. OK, let's try those!"

Sophie and I spent the next hour solving puzzles using gravity and portal devices. She was funny, insightful, intelligent, and just great to spend time with.

"Careful," Billby didn't suggest.

"Uh, I better go, Sophie. Need to make cook. Food, cook food."

"Aww! But I'm having fun! Well, don't forget about next week's poetry club. I'm sure it'll be fun, with our spooky theme."

"Ask her!" Billby demanded.

"Uh, why Eldritch horrors and, uh, obscure Deities? It's August."

"Never too early to get into the Halloween spirit, Prawn! You should see my cupboard. All sorts of fun, Halloween-themed clothes. Even my undies!" she said with a giggle.

Fudge. Didn't want to start thinking about that again. I was still reeling from the bloody cheesecake tank top yesterday.

"Coward," Billby didn't mock.

"Oh, um, I love Halloween. Best, favourite holiday. OK, bye Sophie."

"Bye, Prawnstar!"

I breathed deep, closing my eyes, as the call ended. Turned to face Billby, silently judging me from the desk.

"I can judge you out loud if you prefer, mate?" Billby taunted.

Sure, why not. Let's hear what crackpot theories he has this time.

"Honestly, Prawn, I'm beginning to wonder if I'm wrong."

Uh... what?

"Really. She's sweet. Kind. Smart. Incredibly bloody smart, actually. Way too smart to be an estate agent, don't you think?"

"Huh... yeah, actually. She could easily be a scientist or doctor or something, or—"

"Yeah, exactly. And how quickly she solved those puzzles, for someone who never played but just so happened to own the Portal games? She's skilled, too. Clearly an analytical and critical thinker."

Yeah... she was. Very smart and... analytical.

"Well, I'm not suggesting I'm completely crazy here, Prawn. But you're a smart kid yourself, mate. Eyes open, yeah?"

Yeah.

"Thanks, Billby."

I gave my bear a big hug before setting him back down on the desk again. Time to go check on Badger and Violet, finally go delve into the space heisting malarkey I think.

"Not hungry?" Billby asked.

Nope.

"Liar."

Fudge.

Phone buzzed. Sophie.

"Had a lovely time, Prawnstar. Let's do it again tomorrow."

Felt myself cracking a smile, staring at the text.

"Was that a question, or an order?" Billby helpfully suggested.

Fudge, it didn't feel like an obligation. It was something I wanted to do, and liked the idea of.

"Like the idea of her Halloween undies? Or her watermelon cheesecake? Or her red robes, ritualistic dagger and altar sacrifices?"

"Now you sound crazy, Billby," I snapped. "She's not a recruiter, not using her body as a weapon, not trying to control me, not—"

"More knots than a bloody sailor's rope, mate. Listen to yourself. I'm not suggesting she's going to carve your heart out on an altar here, but you need to at least consider your safety. You've barely known her five minutes, Prawn. You're smarter than this, mate."

I sighed deep, staring at the server, Jester, Violet and Badger already online. Somehow, didn't feel like joining them right now.

Went and slumped on the sofa, staring at the word tomorrow. All it needed was one little question mark, but it was loud, overbearing in its absence.

Fudge.

Chapter 11 - DANGER

Thursday was poetry club, Friday I gamed with the Sophinator, and today I'm supposed to play again, but I can't. Found a note, slipped under my door in the night.

"Finally," Billby didn't say, as I held the note in my hand.

The note, slipped under my door, staring into me as I stared at it.

Flat 6. Midnight. DANGER.

"Sit down," Billby commanded.

Tried. Legs were jelly. Tears welling. Hands shaking. Almost felt like Billby dragged me to the sofa himself.

Collapsed onto it, staring at the note—the letters seemed to dance, assemble into a figure, a figure pointing, laughing.

Pointing.

Laughing.

"Danger," Billby stated plainly. "Will you FINALLY start listening to me?"

Fudge.

"Settle down, Prawn," Billby said. "Breathe, mate. Right, let's think. Be smart, be safe. Who could have slipped this under your door? Why? Who even is in flat six?"

That was a good question. Ground floor was Sophie and myself, then upstairs... hmm. Ahmed, his wife Zara and their baby. James and Denise. Karen. Had I—had I ever actually MET the last resident?

No. No, I hadn't. Nobody had. She redefines the word hermit—all deliveries arrive at her flat through some kind of shutter chute thing, opens and closes out of the door. I know her name is Samantha, but that's all I know.

Could she have given me the note? Or... Sophie? Is she trying to warn me?

"Think, Prawn. What's more likely—the safe, secure, clued-up Samantha or the, uh... well, Sophie. You tell me which seems safer."

How was I supposed to get through today with this looming over me? I wasn't hungry, wasn't thirsty, couldn't focus or even breathe—I just—

"Settle down already, Prawn. Bloody annoying, mate," Billby mocked. "Just go game."

Now there was an idea. Why not call Badger, tell him about the note? Or... do I ask Sophie then?

"Yeah, think that through, mate. 'Hi cult recruiter lady with the massive melons, I got a note here saying you're dangerous.' That's smart, isn't it, mate."

"Can you stop commenting on her bloody... chest!" I snapped at Billby.

He pointed at me and laughed from his spot on the desk.

No. No he didn't. He just sat there, staring at me, blank lifeless face as ever. Settle down, Prawn.

I wanted to just tear the note up, chuck it in the bin and forget about it. Move on, go play, hang out with my friends. Some weekend respite from my work.

"Can't though, can you, mate? It's still in your hand."

Looked at the note again. Danger.

Phone buzzed, fumbled in my pocket for it. Sophie.

"You've been quiet, mister! We playing today or what? Soph xx"

"Do it," Billby didn't suggest.

Wait, what?

"Not like you to suggest that? What happened to your spiel about danger and safety and cults and—"

"Settle down, mate. She can gather intel, so can you. Get her talking. Loosen her up a little, give her a probing. Find out what she knows."

Shook the imagery from my head. Not actually a bad idea. Maybe I can play with Sophie, and ask a few simple, curious questions. Nothing more than... oh. Wait.

Sophie's barely lived here a few weeks? If that. She'll know nothing about Samantha.

"Good point. Waste of time, then," Billby suggested.

Well, if I was going to waste some time today, why not with a good friend.

"Good recruiter," Billby helpfully added.

"Dearest Sophie, I—"

"Mate, you from the Victorian era? Try again. Was less embarrassed for you when you nearly opened your door with no trousers on."

Thanks, Billby. Love you too. Bloody bear.

Deleted that. Try again.

"Sophie, why don't you join me, we can—"

"Just text her a picture of your banana, mate."

...

"Are you trying to help me or sabotage me here, Billby?"

"Sorry, sorry. Don't do that. Just text back 'let's go'. Two words. Nice, easy, simple, just like you."

"Let's go." Nice, easy, simple. Yeah. That was fine. Sent it and waited.

Buzz.

"I'm online! Come on then. More puzzles?"

"Yep."

Hopped online, joined Sophie on the voice chat.

"Hi Prawn! Didn't interrupt your phone call, did I?"

Huh? What phone call?

"Uh, hi, um, no? I'm not—I wasn't on the phone."

"Oh! Could swear I heard your voice. Maybe you were talking to your telly. I do that too, don't worry. Puzzles, then?"

That was odd.

We hopped back onto our puzzle game and spent the next hour enjoying the process.

After some time, I decided to ask a couple of questions anyway, just in case she could help.

"Um, Sophie? Have you met the girl in flat six?"

"Samantha? Nope! Only Karen has. Why?"

Oh fudge! I didn't think that far ahead. Why would I want to know that?

"Curious," Billby helpfully suggested.

"Oh, just curious."

"Understandable! Nobody has seen her. We're all a little curious. Bit creepy, don't you think? Proper hermit."

"Judgemental," Billby judged.

"Oh, I'm not sure. She seems safe."

"Safety or solitary! Might as well be in prison," Sophie suggested curtly.

Narrowed my gaze at the screen, clenched my fists a little. Seemed a bit...

"Callous? Cold? Cruel? Controlling?"

"That's enough!" I snapped at Billby.

"Prawn? You alright? Enough what? Was I doing the puzzle wrong?" Sophie meekly replied.

"Oh! Oh, no. Um, I was thinking out loud. I'm sorry, ignore me."

"Sure, Prawn. Let me know if you need to talk."

Another hour passed, bit quieter than the one before. Sophie hopped off to head to town, shopping.

Spent more time on the sofa, staring at the telly, but not really watching it. Couldn't even remember what I'd seen under duress. Just holding this note as it burned my hand.

"Right then," Billby said. "It's getting late. Soon be showtime. I assume we're going to meet her, yes?"

"Huh? Sophie?"

"No, dipshit. Stop thinking with your banana and use your brain. Samantha, Sammy, the smart one safe in her castle. Had to be her who gave us the note, right? Had to. But tell me something—how'd Sophie know her name?"

I couldn't answer that. I didn't really want to go up there, either. Even if I did, she had never answered the door for anyone, at all, ever. Not even once.

"You've been invited into her inner sanctum. You have to be brave, Prawn. You can do this."

"I'm... I'm scared," I mumbled gently.

"I know you are. But you got me, and I'm here to keep you safe. Always will. Eat, drink, get ready."

Was gone eleven, and the last hour felt like it would take an eternity. Every agonising minute excruciating. Phone buzzed, Sophie again.

"Had fun today Prawn. Got you a treat from town! Come get it tomorrow? Soph xx"

I smiled wide, seeing the question mark. Billby was wrong, she was just—

"Just."

Fudge.

71

Midnight in ten minutes, checking the time on my phone. Hands betrayed me, shaking like bowls of jelly.

"Bet you wish Soph—"

"Don't even bloody start, Billby."

Cut him off before he could be crude. Bloody bear needed therapy.

"You're the one imagining me, muppet."

I'm ignoring that.

"No you're not. Can feel you about to cry. Grow the fuck up already."

"Billby!"

"No, mate. Fudge this, fudge that. Fucking juvenile. You don't even eat the bloody stuff, nitwit."

Tossed Billby onto the sofa, and grabbed a protein bar. Had to eat something. Not even sure I've had breakfast today, come to think of it.

"Nope. You're slipping."

Fudge.

Right. Two minutes to midnight. Sweat dripping down my brow as I slowly, carefully opened my door. Darkness in the looming corridor, heart pounding out of my chest.

Can't do this.

"Must."

Slowly pulled my door shut, quietly clicked. Light on under Sophie's door—she was still up? Well, guess it was a weekend.

Slowly made my way up the stairs, one foot after another, hoping, praying nobody would hear or see me.

"Wait!" Billby whispered. "Did you forget your trousers again?"

Hurriedly grabbed at my legs, sighing as I felt cloth, before slowly continuing.

Used the light from my phone to guide me as I reached the landing.

There they were. Two flats on my left, two my right, one at the back corner—Samantha.

Approached her door. It was pitch black, and... her door was ajar, ever so slightly. A faint blue glow came from the doorway.

Clutched Billby tight to my chest, and placed my shaking hand on the door.

"Wait!" Billby whispered as my hand hovered. "Bit late, but, what if she's the cult leader?"

Fudge.

"Don't worry actually mate. I know bear-jitsu."

Great. Waltzing into a lion's den with a stuffed bear as my backup. Just bloody perfect.

Fud—fuck.

Chapter 12 - Naked

Heart hammering in my ears as I gently pushed the door open. My hand shook like a jackhammer.

"Prawn, you're making ME nervous. Settle down!" Billby said.

Blue glow cast across the entrance from a series of monitors. Sammy sat in front of them, before standing and—

OH DEAR FUCKING GOD!

WHAT THE ACTUAL FUCK!

SHE'S FUCKING—

SHE'S—

"Stark. Bollock. NAKED," Billby muttered.

YEAH. *THAT.*

"Peter Ross Awning. Sammy. Close the door. Quickly," Sammy muttered.

Pulse in my ears. Whole body shaking. Was she— about to hurt me?

"No. Look at her, Prawn," Billby stated.

Oh, fudge. He's right.

Eyes, twitching. Hair, unkempt, unwashed, down to her knees. Fear was painted across her face along with the remnants of her dinner.

"You. I watch you," Sammy said, taking a step closer.

Pressed myself nervously against the door, hand trembling on the handle.

"I have the cameras. They're with me. You're onto them, aren't you? Like me. You see it too. I know you do."

Billby... help... should we run?

"Forget the melons and the birds' nest, mate. Pay attention. This is serious. More serious than anything else so far. Eyes up, mate. Listen."

"Bet you thought you were crazy," Sammy continued. "I've been watching. Observing. Listening. There's a CULT here. I've seen it. We're in terrible danger."

Oh... fudge. Oh fudge. Ohfudgeohfudgeoh—

"Hey! Snap to it, Prawn," Billby jabbed.

Right. Settle down. Focus. Bloody hell, is that what they look like?

"Prawn. Not bloody now, mate. Eyes up."

Right.

"Ahem, um, well, what do you mean? Also, uh, don't you have, err, clothes?"

"Of course not!" Sammy snapped. "They use them to control you. Admit it. You wore the shirt, and you felt different, didn't you? I watched you all. I've got cameras in the halls, the communal room, the lobby—I see it all."

Fuck. I did. I felt very different, wearing the shirt. Like part of a group, part of a... a...

"Cult," Billby didn't finish.

"Karen is their leader. Always has been. Once a month, knocks on my door. Every month, without fail. I never answer."

I gazed over at the monitors. They were the only things providing light in the entire room—guessing she never turned on the bulb.

She wasn't well. She was... wrong.

"Wisdom and insanity sometimes look like the same thing, Prawn," Billby said. "Hear her out. If she's batshit, we'll fly right outta here like bats outta hell."

"Um, what exactly have you seen that—"

"Ever been in the storage room, Peter? Didn't think so. Only Karen has the key. She's preparing for phase two."

"Um... phase... phase two?"

Sammy gestured for me to follow and look at the monitors.

"Basement—just a laundry room, right? WRONG. The storage cupboard is where they take them."

"Um... take... take who?"

"The... chosen."

I can't listen to this. My breathing shallow, my pulse fast, my head spinning, my—

"Settle down!" Billby snapped.

"You'll see. You will. I'm not safe, Peter. Nobody is."

"Um... who is, uh, if we're not in the cult, then—"

"You want to know if the girl is. The one you like."

Fudge! Was it—was it that obvious?

"Bloody Martians can see it, mate," Billby mocked.

Ugh.

"She's... there's something off with her. But I'm not telling you tonight. I need to know more. You have to go now. My head hurts. I need to sleep. Unless you want to join me? Safer. We can sleep head to toe."

Dear fucking Christ, no.

"Agreed," Billby stated simply.

"Um, gotta go. Uh, bye."

"Midnight. After the next 'poetry club'. Come see me again. Leave."

Barely remember stumbling back to my flat. Breathing still shallow and rapid, sat on my sofa, clutching Billby tight against my chest like a shield.

Chapter 13 - Off

Sat on the sofa, staring at the telly. Wasn't on, nor was the light. Just... stared.

Billby hadn't said a word. Sat on my lap, watching that blank screen right along with me.

Darkness felt comforting, somehow. Must be nearly one in the morning.

Sammy's twitching eyes, unkempt features and naked body burned under my eyelids—unwelcome intruders, robbing me of sleep or will.

Say something, Billby.

Nothing.

Just stared back at me, lifeless face.

Closed my eyes, tried to shut out her face, her eyes, her everything.

"Insane, Prawn. She's completely and totally insane," Billby began. "And yet, might be the most sane of us all."

Slumped further back in the sofa, frowning at the blank television in the dark. Didn't have the fight. Couldn't keep arguing with Billby, when all he wanted to do was keep me safe.

But, I wasn't ready to trust the word of a crazy woman.

"Not suggesting you convert to her church, mate," Billby said. "But it wouldn't be wise, or safe, to just ignore everything she said. Do the work, sort the wheat from the chaff."

Couldn't. So damn fudging tired. Just wanted to sleep. Crawled into bed and stared at the ceiling, waiting for it to say something, or fall.

"Ignorant," Billby didn't mock.

"Huh?"

"Already back to thinking about melons and cheesecakes, when you've just been given PROOF she's in a cult."

"Proof? What are—"

"She used the word 'off', Prawn. Not quirky, or different, or unusual. Not interesting, or unique, or special. No. Off."

Off. Off.

"You can interpret all those other words to mean anything. They have ambiguity. But off? Opposite of on, mate. Right and wrong, on and off. Get your head out of that cheesecake and wake up already."

"Billby, it's nearly two in the morn—"

"Oh, fair play, mate. Didn't know cult danger slept through the night. My bad—go count sheep and I'll keep an eye on your kidneys for you."

Can't think about this tonight. So tired. Need sleep—

"Need a sense of survival, mate. Get handed proof you've joined a bloody CULT and your mind is off thinking about HER. You're pathetic."

No, not fair. She's clearly insane! She was all kinds of disturbed. I can't trust her any more than I can anyone else in the building.

"See? We agree on that. Difference is, she's smart."

"She's got a screw loose, Billby!"

"She's got no screws or marbles left, mate. Chucked them out with her clothes. But you can't be naive enough to judge a book by the cover, mate. You aren't with Sophie, so why with Sammy?"

Hm. Fair question, actually.

"Biases, mate. You're more likely to accept truths given by an angel than a demon. Sophie's cult comes wrapped in an attractive package. Sammy's light comes shrouded in darkness. Think."

Glared at the ceiling. So damn tired. Did my bloody bear actually have a point? Or was he being even more pedantic than usual?

"Don't make this about me, Prawn. I'm a stuffed bear, mate—not exactly special. Make it about being safe."

Safety. Solitary.

"Great, using Sophie's words like cult programming. You're a good little convert, aren't you, Prawn? Make sure to write a nice poem for Thursday when you summon Cthulhu. Think they'll let you hold the ritual dagger?"

No! Let me sleep!

"Why? You think you deserve to pull the wool over your eyes and sleep this away? No, mate. Face it—you're a cultist, and you're in danger."

Danger. No! No?

"Yo—you! You're the danger!"

"Like I said, stuffed bloody bear, mate. Bit of a fire hazard, all this fur, but that's the only danger you'll see from me. Can't exactly grip the ritual dagger now, can I?"

Suppose not. But I did grin wide thinking about Billby wearing a cute little red robe.

"Mate, I'd look so adorable. Plus, how cute I am? Better recruiter than Sophie, mate. Think Karen has any job openings?"

Lay there, chuckling away with Billby. Think I needed that after a roller coaster of a day.

"Look, Prawn, just get some rest, mate. You're a cranky git when you're tired. Well, more than normal, I mean. Love you, mate."

"Love you, Billby. Watch over me whilst I sleep?"

"Always have, always will, mate."

Finally closed my eyes, smile on my face, utterly and completely exhausted.

Chapter 14 - But

Thank God it was Sunday. It's gone midday, staring at my phone screen, and I'm still under the covers.

"Warm. Safe."

Barely wanted to leave, but luckily it was socially acceptable to lounge around on a Sunday.

"Lazy git, mate," Billby jested.

Fine, fine. Dragged myself out of bed, too late for breakfast. Guess a protein bar will do for lunch.

Phone buzzed—Sophie.

"Hiya Prawn! I've got a new game for Prawnstar to play. Interested? Soph xx"

Felt myself smile, staring at the screen.

"Hopefully it's not disassemble the chosen victims' body, mate," Billby helpfully added.

Bloody bear. Bears are meant to be furry, not snarky.

"Hah! Fudge, Prawn. That was bloody hilarious. Give up that fraud investigation malarkey, mate—you're a stand-up comedian."

"Much prefer sitting, Billby!"

Felt myself chuckling, giving Billby a hug.

"Mate. Better reply to Sophinator, hadn't you. Still think you should try that banana—"

"Billby."

Right. Texts. Games. Hmm.

"Dearest Soph—"

"Prawn, mate. Settle down. Christ."

Right, right.

"Yep."

There. Sent. Nice and simple.

"Hold on, Prawn. Didn't you want more info first? What if the game is hide the dagger in the initiate's ribs?"

Fudge.

"Why couldn't you bloody tell me that BEFORE I sent it?"

"Now where's the fun in that?" Billby teased.

"Are you here to help me or hinder me, sodding bear!"

"That should be obvious. But I'm not omnipotent, mate—I don't catch everything you miss."

Which means he doesn't miss everything I catch, either?

"Prawn, mate, what does that even mean? Settle down."

Fudge. Hadn't even realised Sophie had replied. Tapped the screen.

"Great! Come round at four. Poker night at my place!"

Oh. Oh FUDGE.

"She nailed you to the bloody altar there, mate. Nice going."

"B-but, she said a game—a game, not a—"

"A game? You mean like poker, mate?"

FUCK!

"Bloody hell. Language, young man."

No! I'm not about to be scolded by a sodding teddy bear. Oh fudge, I've agreed to go now. Who would think game meant a bloody poker night! What the fudge!

"She's bloody smart, Prawn. Or off, if you will. That's a better descriptor."

Off. Something off.

Fudge it. Pit in my stomach, hands shaking, telly laughing at me. But I made the commitment now. Besides, it was just poker—what's the worst that can happen?

"Cultist orgies, sacrificial rituals, summoning Eldritch—"

"THANK YOU, Billby."

Fudge.

Deep breath, check the time. An hour to prepare.

"Just game," Billby suggested. "Relax. I'll keep you safe."

An hour passed, and my hand shook as I held my door handle. I wanted to bring something, but I couldn't figure out what, and didn't seem to have enough hands.

The hallway loomed ahead, bright and disturbing. Could already hear voices inside.

"More people, more problems," Billby said, appearing in my left hand.

Hand hovered above the door. I could leave. Just go back to my flat. Text that I've got a cold.

"She'd bring you soup," Billby stated.

Yeah. Tried to escape social obligations before, and that ended up with her nearly entering the inner sanctum. Couldn't have that.

"Agreed."

Swallowed hard, closed my eyes and knocked on the door.

"Prawn! There he is," Marcus beamed as he opened the door. Bright, cheerful green eyes greeting me as warmly as his smile.

"Oh, uh, hi all," I mumbled, feeling myself smile as I stepped inside.

Bright, colourful, messy—but full of flavour. Character. Humanity.

"Deception," Billby didn't helpfully suggest.

"Greetings, Peter," Ali said with a wave, sat at the table. Poker chips and cards were splayed all over it, a true mess, but it was somehow beautiful.

"Yay! The Prawnstar himself!" Sophie cheered, rushing up to give me a hug. Warm, soft, kind. Same cheesecake tank top as before, happy smile complimenting her own.

"Complimenting something else too," Billby didn't crudely imply.

Sat at the table, and let Ali explain the rules. I'd played before, but honestly forgotten. Marcus brought a pizza from work, too. I could get used to this, I think.

"Psst, Prawn," Billby whispered. "I can see. Sophie has a good pair."

Nice. I did too—queens. Pair of what though, Billby?

"Melons!"

Fudge. NOT funny, Billby. You're being cruel, and objectifying, and—wait. Wait.

You're compartmentalising my feelings for her down to simple physical attraction. You're deflecting me from the truth with crudeness.

I like her.

That moment, almost felt like I was somewhere else. A dark room, sat on a chair, surrounded by... Billby. He was everywhere and nowhere, visibly frowning.

"Yeah. You got me. Can't deny it, Prawn. I know you like her, I can feel it. But I'm worried she's going to break your heart, just like he did."

The cable. The n—

"Don't," Billby commanded. "Don't go there. Just... be careful. Be safe. Can't lose you, like we lost him."

"Prawn?" Sophie said, as I snapped back to the table.

"Oh, um, I'm, uh, ALL IN!"

Pushed my chips to the middle of the table. Fudge it, why not.

"You... you didn't even look at your cards," Sophie stammered.

Grinned wide. Reached my eyes.

"T-taking a chance. All in."

"Nope. Fold. Too impressed by the stones on this one," Marcus said, cards dropped on the table with a satisfying plop.

"Allah guides him. Fold," Ali agreed with a grin.

Sophie giggled. "Nope. Far too impressed. I'm folding too. Who are you and what have you done with Prawn?"

Sophie fanned herself dramatically. Had to chuckle at that, the light above reflecting from the emerald green of her eyes.

I won the round, and didn't even look at my cards. Was there a lesson here?

"Risk," Billby didn't jab.

"Come on, fella, you gotta show us what you got," Marcus politely asked.

"You, uh, you know what?" I responded. "Nah. Shuffle them back in. Some stuff I don't need to know."

"Blind," Billby didn't warn.

Rest of poker night was full of warmth, laughs, and the rest of that delicious pizza that I thankfully didn't have to order myself. I could get used to poker night happening again. Maybe even regularly.

Back home, sat on my sofa, smiling at the blank telly. Didn't really feel a need to watch anything, just sit and breathe.

"Well done," Billby began. "You did well."

"What do you mean?"

"They're buying it. You're in, one of them. Under the hooded robe."

"I... I—"

"You've got some guts, Prawn. Didn't know you had it in you. I'm genuinely impressed. But."

But? But. But...

"Bit convenient, isn't it? Just so happens to move in next door at the right time, age appropriate, single, gamer. Smart, cute, and don't even get me started on those—"

"Billby."

"You get my point. I'm not disrespecting you, Prawn— you're a great guy. You know I'm here to keep you safe. But the timing, the interest, doesn't any of it feel at all... convenient?"

Shook my head fiercely. Wasn't listening to this.

"If I noticed, you noticed. Sophie wants herself a Prawn salad, mate. She's into you."

"She... she is?"

"Saw the way she looked at you, mate. Even I could see it and I'm a bloody teddy bear. But that shouldn't be making you feel happy. Should make you feel pause."

Flash of Sammy appeared in my mind, frown curling down. Was Billby right?

But tonight was... warm. Kind. Fun, genuine. Real affection, real connection, real—

"Real good acting. Real evidence. Real cult. Real smooth."

No... no... no?

"Maybe I'm being a bit harsh, Prawn. But maybe there's more to this than you realise, and we both know that."

Maybe. Maybe there was.

Fudge.

Chapter 15 - Bear

Today was the day. Blinked through the week at work—sorry to hear that, sir, your claim has been declined, sir, no, sir, you can't claim you were scammed because you dropped your ice cream cone sir.

Another terrible performance review too. Sometimes wondered why they bothered with those—could all be done through an email. Doesn't matter how hard you try, always something you're doing wrong, or they want doing better.

Still. Enjoying my evenings, hanging out online with the guild or Sophinator. Haven't introduced them yet—not with the... issues, still persisting.

Been researching poetry. Rather research poker tactics, but I'm coming up with a poem for tonight's poetry club.

"And counter-cult club with Sammy, mate."

Sighed, slumping in my chair. Almost forgot about that. Her twitching eyes, unkempt hair, and... lack of clothes... ugh.

"Truth can be ugly, mate."

Still. I'd written 'Artaois', my poem about the Celtic bear god. Obscure enough for poetry club's 'Obscure Deities and Eldritch Horrors' theme, I hope.

"Flattering," Billby whispered.

Please. Wrote about a bear god, not a bear bellend.

"Ain't got one, mate. Stuffed bear, remember. Speaking of remember, where's your cult robe?"

Fudge! The shirt. Still balled up in the corner of the sofa where I left it. Surprised I hadn't noticed—stood out against the rest of my tidy flat like a sore thumb.

"Red as blood too, mate. Slipping."

Could always count on Billby to keep me safe. Sane, on the other hand—

"Very bloody funny. Wins a round of poker and thinks he's hot stuff. Settle down."

Could already hear people gathering in the communal room as I pulled on my uniform. Knock at my door?

Breathed deep and reached for the handle, gripping it tight.

"Hi Prawn!" Sophie beamed, stood in the looming hallway. 'Bear the Word' shirt on, glaring at me with that crimson red.

"Um, hi? You OK?"

"Yep! Just thought I'd walk you and the bear to poetry. Guess he's kind of our mascot, isn't he?"

"Wait a minute, Prawn—am I the cult leader now? Gonna need to order me a tiny little red robe and a dagger, mate. No, start me off small actually—I'll take a butter knife."

Shook Billby out and followed Sophie as she—uh.

Held my hand? Held my hand. My hand. Held.

HELD MY HAND.

Pulse pounding in my ears, shaking, sweat on my brow.

"It's OK, Prawn—we're here now! Hi everyone!" Let me go and went to sit down.

Karen, James and Denise sat on one side of the table. Ali, Sophie and I the other. There was a nervous energy in the air, for some reason.

"Check this out," Karen said, turning off the light and presenting a large wax candle.

"Fairly sure that's a f-fire hazard," James stammered.

"But thematic," Ali added. "I approve."

Dim light from the candle flickered in the room, casting light and shadow on the walls. Clutched Billby a little tighter.

"Got you, Prawn," he didn't say.

"Can I go first, Karen? Please?" Denise pleaded.

"Sure! We're all equals here," Karen gently suggested.

Glared at the dancing candle, chest feeling tight. Maybe that were true.

Maybe.

Light flickered as Denise cleared her throat, poem in her hand.

"Ahem, this poem is about Azathoth, the supreme deity. Bear witness:

Idiot drums upon a throne, dreams the cosmos we call our home.

Hearing the words in my ears, I felt myself clutch Billby even tighter. What... what was that?

"Prawn, I'm scared," Billby didn't whisper.

Me too, buddy. Me too.

"Insightful," Ali stated. "So, should he wake, does reality cease?"

"What makes you say that?" Karen enquired.

"Well, if the cosmos is his dream, then does reality end when he wakes? Think of our own dreams, as Allah calls us from them each day."

"Hmm," Denise began. "I much prefer the idea of an ordered and caring deity, than a blind idiot drumming us into existence from an endless throne."

"What do you think, Prawn?" Sophie suggested, gently stroking my arm as I quivered.

"Oh, um, I, um, I wrote one. Something, I mean. About the Celtic bear god, Artaois."

Sophie clapped. "Oh, how lovely! Can we hear it?"

Placed Billby on the table, and stared right into his lifeless face. Took a deep breath, closed my eyes, and let the words free.

Bear the comfort, bear the chain, bear the darkness, bear the pain.

Silence. Nobody saying a word. All staring at me, or the candle, or Billby, or—

"B-brave," James stuttered.

"Profound. We must all bear our burdens, inshallah," Ali agreed.

"Well done, Prawn! Inspired by our furry little mascot, here," Sophie cheered, before—oh no.

Oh, what has she done. Oh, no, no, no.

She picked up Billby and hugged him. Felt my body shake as she did, sweat beading on my brow. I need him back. He won't like this. I'm not going to hear the end of this. Oh fudge.

"Um, th-thanks," I mumbled, grabbing Billby back with perhaps a touch too much force.

Sophie smiled warmly. "Right then. My turn!"

Poems and discussion exchanged for another half hour, until finally the club was concluded.

Locked my door tight, deadbolt too, and slumped against it. Billby stank of strawberry perfume.

"Proud of you, Prawn," Billby gently said.

...What?

"Stayed strong throughout that. Wrote a poem that played your part flawlessly. You're in, one of the cult. Now we know who they worship, does that give us any power? Are we safe?"

"I... I don't honestly know. Um, you aren't mad about the hug?"

"I smell great! Who doesn't love strawberries? Not that a stuffed bear can eat them," Billby jested.

Stared into the dark, slumped against the floor. Think my frown about joined my butt on the carpet. Why was I feeling so...

"Empty? Hollow? Defeated, deflated, depressed?" Billby asked. "Because your night ain't over, mate. It's only just begun."

Chapter 16 - NO

Midnight approached. I was chewing a pen, but I'm currently staring at it in two halves on the carpet.

Can't do this.

"Must."

Billby, I—

"Look how far you've come, Prawn. Everything we've been through together so far—you think I'm scared of a little cult?"

I... no. You're the brave one. You always have been.

"Right. So let me be brave with you now. Sammy spent the past week finding out what we need. Told us Sophie is off, and Karen has been knocking on her door every month. We must know."

"Must we? Why is it our business? Can't we just—"

"I hear your words, but I see your thoughts, too. I see her green eyes, her beautiful siren song smile. The voice, heavenly like an angel, whilst her words spew from your lips."

He was wrong. He... he had to be.

"Sorry, mate. I wish I was wrong, that I was half as crazy as Sammy is and isn't. But I'm not, am I? You know I'm right."

Couldn't stand admitting it, but the evidence was mounting. How much longer could I close my—

Wait.

Breathed in, deep, counted to ten and stilled my mind. Eyes closed, ten, open.

WHAT evidence?

What actually, factually has happened that in any way screams "Cult!"?

... Nothing? Nothing. Nothing!

"NO!" Billby roared, furious as a savage lion tearing apart a doe—hungry, ravenous, starving. "The shirts. The poems. The recruit—"

No, no, no, no, no, no, NONONO!

STOP IT, Billby!

You're WRONG!

"I'M NOT WRONG!" Billby roared once more. Dropped to my knees, tears rushing to the thirsty carpet below. Whole body shaking. Sophie's smile, her eyes, her gentle touch—

"Ah. But there it is. I see it, Prawn, clear as crystal. You love her. But beyond that? You FEAR her. I see it. I feel it. I live it."

Please, Billby... please, stop. Please.

"I don't need to say another word, Prawn. Your fear tastes like poison."

Fuck it. Fuck.

So fucking tired. Fine.

"You win, Billby. Let's go see your nutterbutter whackadoodle girlfriend."

"Finally. You're bloody difficult, mate, you know that? Actually, don't respond. Just fucking get up off the carpet already, pull yourself together and move."

Door open, darkness. Sammy probably watching on the hallway camera.

Checked and made sure I had trousers on. Knew I did, but felt important.

Looked at Sophie's door. Walked over to it. Light on, still up.

"Can't," Billby said simply.

Lip quivered, tears rushed down my cheeks. I needed her.

But.

I needed Billby more.

Clenched my fists tight, slowly started up the stairs to the landing, and—

Wait.

Something is wrong.

VERY wrong.

Sammy's door—wide open, light on.

Sobbing inside, as I felt my feet shuffle themselves, one after the other, closer and closer to the door.

"Prawn... I'm scared," Billby admitted.

Yep.

Step into the open doorway.

Karen.

Hunched over, crying, sobbing over Sammy.

Dead Sammy.

"Murdered Sammy," Billby whispered.

Fuck.

Chapter 17 - RUN

"Prawn. Prawn. PRAWN!" Billby yelled, ringing hollow in my ears. "We NEED to go. That's a CORPSE, Prawn."

Legs, shaking. Arms, shaking. Everything shaking.

Karen, hunched over Sammy, on her knees and sobbing. Phone in her hand, call on the screen.

"PRAWN! LEAVE!" Billby didn't roar.

"P... Pete... Peter, is that you?" Karen sobbed through tears, spotting me frozen in the doorway.

"MOVE, PRAWN! RUN! FUCKING RUN, PRAWN, RUN, RUN, RUN, R—"

No use. I could hear him, but I also couldn't. So grey. Pale. Just like—just like last time—

"STOP!" Billby roared.

Shook my head. Karen stood, sobbing hard. Rushed over to me.

Didn't feel the knife as it pierced my chest. Felt her arms around my back instead, crying her eyes out, phone held in her hand. Stood there, paralysed. Can't move. Think. Breathe.

No sirens, but the blue lights were just as loud. Flashed in from the window on the landing, end of the hallway.

Karen and I to the side, staring. Watching. Covered Sammy, gave her back some dignity.

Ringing in my ears all through the next three hours. Didn't hear a word. Didn't see a thing. Found myself on her sofa, head in her lap, gently sobbing. How I got here, couldn't say. Where I'd go, didn't know.

"Shh. I've got you, Prawn," Sophie muttered, gently stroking my hair as I sobbed.

The smile was gone from her voice. The light, from her eyes. The bubbly, fun, sweet girl that I lo—

That I—

Gone. Yet not. Just... stroking. Comforting me or herself, didn't know. Didn't care.

Chapter 18 - Snakes

Woke up some time later, on Sophie's sofa. She'd gone, but wasn't sure where. A few blissful moments of ignorance passed as I came to my senses, shaking off the grog.

Fudge. Sammy went kerblammy. Dead as a dodo.

Frowned, clenching my fists. Shouldn't have tried to joke my way past this. Not fair to Sammy, or myself.

Where was Sophie? And—oh.

Oh no.

Where was... Billby?

Oh FUCK.

Began to breathe, hard. Visions of a simple, yellow ethernet cable popped into my head. Slithered under the door, like a python, or a cobra, or a boa or a—

Quick! Think of more snakes! I NEED MORE SNAKES!

"Prawn?" Sophie pushed open the door as I shook violently on her sofa. There he was, Billby, sat against her chest, head buried.

"S-Sophie," I stammered.

She rushed over to me, handing me back Billby. Hugged him tight, shield against the snakes.

Breathe in, out. Just in, and out. Few more times. There.

"Better?" Billby didn't gently say.

"Prawn, um," Sophie mumbled, frowning. She stared down at the floor. "Can I have a hug?"

Her voice was weak, cracking. Scared? Sad?

"Sadistic," Billby didn't suggest. *"We have to go."*

Shook him away, stood up. Legs were jelly.

"Y-yes. Please."

Sophie threw her arms around me—warm, soft, tight. Billby seemed to get hotter and hotter and hotter as he was wedged between us, until I could bear the heat no longer.

Pulled away and forced on a smile. Looked into her striking, emerald eyes. Full of fear? Failure? F—

"Fraud," Billby didn't jab.

"Prawn, I don't want to be alone. That was scary. You found Karen and Sammy... are you... OK?"

Opened my eyes wide, clutching Billby to my chest. I honestly had no fudging idea.

"Leave," Billby didn't insist.

"Um, I better, maybe go home and—"

Her lip was quivering. Tears started falling from her eyes. Oh.

"Come on!" Billby didn't insist once more.

"I'm scared, Prawn. I think there's a—think there's a c-cult. A cult."

"Wait, what?" Billby and I said.

Nodded her head and wiped away her tears. Sat on her sofa and beckoned me over.

"Danger," Billby warned.

Sat next to her and let her rest her head on my shoulder. After a few minutes, she sat up, straightened her shirt and spoke.

"I found Billby outside Sammy's flat. The door wasn't locked and I... I..."

Looked down at the floor, her hands shaking a little.

"The glow... I was curious. I'm not a bad person, Prawn, I'm not. But I saw the glow and I went inside. She has all these monitors, doesn't she? Did you see them?"

Nodded, but didn't speak. Seemed I needed to listen. On that, Billby and I agreed.gfh vvvvvv

"She has the cameras. Never really questioned who did—just helped me feel safe. But she also had all this... research."

Sophie paused a moment, breathing deep.

"Bear the Word. The Cult of the Bear. These creepy deities she was looking at. Research on mind control and amnesia medication and all sorts. And these... these pictures, Prawn. She had pictures of all of us in these red robes."

Fudge.

"Fuck," Billby whispered.

Time almost seemed to stand still. Sophie wasn't moving, but Billby was. He hovered, right in front of me, frowning.

"You realise what this means? I was... actually right. Red robes, pictures, evidence. You thought I was crazy. I thought I was crazy. But I was right."

Shaking. Bile in my throat. Sprinted back to my flat, didn't even hear Sophie protest. Threw up in the toilet.

"Get back in there," Billby demanded. "Hear her words."

Nope. No. No way in hell. Not doing it.

Oh fuck. Found myself opening Sophie's door, her eyes red-rimmed, frowning at me.

"Prawn, I'm scared."

"Don't be," Billby said. "I'm here to keep you safe."

"Thanks, Prawn," Sophie responded, rushing over and giving me a big, warm hug.

Wait. What happened? Did I—did I miss something, here?

Felt like I hadn't slept in the longest time. Even my tired was tired. Where was Billby?

Oh, in my hand. Right.

"I don't know what to do. This is crazy," Sophie admitted. "We're not in a cult. We would know, right?"

Of course we'd know! We're just flat tenants with a poetry club.

"I don't own any robes. Do you?" I asked, confident and resolved.

"Um, no... I guess not?" Sophie replied. "So, how does she have the pictures?"

"She was, uh, well, crazy. Did you take them?" I asked.

Sophie pulled out her phone, hand shaking as she flicked through them. Us all in red hooded robes, Billby too. What the fudge?

"I can't believe it. I'd r-remember," I protested.

Wouldn't I?

"Pictures worth thousands of beared words, mate," Billby suggested.

Fudge. Sure looked convincing. But I would definitely remember that.

"Like you remember carrying me everywhere?" Billby mocked.

Ah fudge. Yeah. That was a thing, wasn't it.

I sighed deep, staring at Sophie. She'd gone and slumped over on her sofa. Barely felt like five minutes ago we were having pizza and poker night at the table nearby.

I can't buy into this cult bullshit. It doesn't make any sense. There had to be a simple, logical explanation for all this.

I got it!

"S-Sophie. Um, let's go back to Sammy's flat. We can find out more."

Sophie looked up at me, managing a brief but wounded smile. "Yeah. Let's do it, Prawn. There's a rational explanation for all this, I'm sure."

Hand shook as I offered it to Sophie. She smiled wide, taking it, rising from her sofa. Quickly let go, searching for Billby.

"Left hand, nitwit," he kindly added.

Bloody bear. Guess we were off to Sammy's flat, then. Hopefully Karen hadn't locked it yet, or we might have to figure out another way inside.

Chapter 19 - Spaghetti

"So, how are we doing this?" Sophie asked tentatively.

Fair question, really. I checked Sammy's flat, and Karen had since locked it. Only way to get inside was somehow pick the lock, maybe? Or some kind of elaborate key heist.

"Prawn?"

"Uh, sorry, Sophie. Just... considering."

Hmm. There's an access near the—

"No, no, no," Billby interrupted. "I know what to do."

Oh fudge. The heck did he have planned? Tear gas? Actual fire? Bulldozer? Velociraptor?

"Just follow me already," Billby beckoned.

Yeah, one problem with that, Billby—you're a stuffed bear.

Felt myself chuckling, despite everything.

"Prawn? What's funny?" Sophie asked, glaring a little.

Maybe not the best time for humour.

Fine, lead on then, Billby. See what kind of hare-brained scheme you've got now. I'll get the fire station number popped in ready to call.

Walked up the stairs, one after the other. Dim evening light cast down the hallway from the small window at the end of the upstairs hall.

Landing seemed smaller now, somehow, with light cast across it.

Walked over to Karen's door, and... knocked on it?

"Peter? That you?" she asked, answering quickly. Sunken eyes, black bags, clearly missing a wink or two.

"Yes. Key to Sammy's please. Dropped something," Billby maybe said.

"Sure."

Fumbled in her pockets for the keys and dropped them in my hand.

That was his master plan? Fudge sake. Bloody bear.

Well, had the key now. Karen shut the door, and I walked over to Sammy's flat. Almost forgot Sophie was in tow, quiet as a church mouse.

Hesitated a moment in front of the door. Somehow seemed dark, almost tainted. Part of me wanted to just go home, go heist a space station with my friends.

"Demoted. Deflated. Defeated."

Thanks, Billby. Bearhole.

He was right, though. Couldn't just waltz downstairs like Sophie hadn't found those pictures. Why didn't Sammy show them to me the first time I visited? Why keep them hidden?

"Bored. Open up," Billby demanded.

Fumbled the key in the lock and turned it. Room looked strange pitch black, shrouded in total darkness. Somehow even creepier without the eerie glaring monitors on and the naked whackadoodle.

Fudge it. Felt tears escaping my eyes again. Can't joke my way out of this, can I, Billby?

"Sorry, mate," Billby said gently.

"Prawn... maybe we don't need to do this? Maybe we just forget it, go downstairs, go game? Prawnstar and Sophinator, sharing our puzzles?"

"Not an option," Billby said. "See it through."

Sophie frowned as I switched on the light. Place was still a decaying mess, a true testament to insanity. Felt the room spinning just looking at the shredded clothes, torn to pieces by hand, the massive pile of empty water bottles, the—

"Focus. Computer," Billby demanded.

Right. Computer on, multiple monitors sparking to life. Sophie stood silent, gently closing the door behind us. Her face was painted with doubt. Did she even want to be here?

"Um, you OK?" I gently asked.

"Prawn... I think we should go. She was mentally ill, Prawn. She cooked this all up in her delusional mind. Let's just go. Come on, you and me. What do you say?"

"NO!" Billby roared.

We turned to the monitors and started clicking through the files. Didn't even notice Sophie leave, or how long it had been since she had, or how many different pictures and files and texts were on this computer.

There we were. Cultist robes, crimson red, hoods. 'Bear the Word.'

Billby hadn't said a word in a long while. Didn't need to.

Huh. Folder named "Peter Ross Awning." I... I can't click on it.

Hands shook, sweat beaded my brow. No, I can't.

"Can't not," Billby said. "I'm with you. Do it."

Clicked it.

Fudge.

There I am, dagger in my hand. Covered in blood. Sammy on the altar, heart removed. But that... that isn't how she died. Is it? No... there wasn't blood. I didn't kill her. I didn't find her. Did I?

"You did. Karen joined you. She started crying," Billby stated.

No... I remember it differently. I came in here and saw Karen sobbing over her corpse. Didn't I?

"No."

Fudge. If I can't trust my own memory, what can I trust?

But the dagger, the blood, the robe—no way. No way in hell.

"Storage cupboard," Billby whispered. "Maybe the robes are in there."

But no, this didn't make any sense. Sammy died up here in this room.

"Unless she was moved."

Fudge. I... didn't consider that. But, there was no blood, right?

"Look down."

Bloodstains on her carpet, clearly visible in the light. But that wasn't there before! I'm sure!

"Prawn, let's go. We need to go."

No. I'm the cult leader. I can go where I please.

"Oh fuck. No, Prawn, no, no. Come on, let's—"

Billby, you'll settle down now. Now fetch me my robe.

"You don't have a—"

Nice try. Go get it.

"Prawn, really, I—"

Going to make me find it myself, am I? Fine, fine. I'll do that. But I'm taking these monitors with me.

"There's dozens!"

Oh, right. Maybe just this empty water bottle then. Seemed important, somehow.

"You really need some fucking sleep, mate. Just close your eyes."

Close my eyes? Didn't feel like it. Felt like I was back on my sofa, key was gone, and I was hungry. How'd I get here?

Had the water bottle, too. Somehow, it mattered.

"Really doesn't! It's a fucking empty bottle, mate!"

Ah, what do you know. You're a sodding teddy bear. Not exactly Oxbridge educated, are you?

Yeah, no reply. That's what I thought.

I'm hungry. Billby, cook me some spaghetti.

"Teddy bear."

Oh. Right.

Pizza! Let's... yeah. Let's do that.

"You are NOT fit to use the phone right now. Get some rest, you're having some kind of—"

"Sorry, sorry, Billby, are you some kind of doctor now? Doctor Bear going to diagnose me with insomnia? How about you shut the fuck up and cook that spaghetti?"

"Still a teddy bear."

Oh. Right.

My head hurt—a lot. I was tired. So, so tired.

"Come on, mate. Been a long couple days. Go lay down. You're not due in work for a while—I already booked your holiday."

Aww, thanks, Billby. No idea how you did that, but thanks. Where are we going? Always wanted to visit Jamaica myself. Just seemed like a cool place to see!

"Fudge have I done. He's lost the plot here. Go. To. Bed. Prawn."

Not going to happen. Not until I get my SPAGHETTI, you evil, sick, vile, cruel teddy bear.

"Literally just a bear mate. You really need to settle down and sleep."

Yeah? Well, YOU need to go and cook me some fucking spaghetti, Billby. I'm hungry.

"Still don't have any hands, Prawn. Shellfish git."

FUCKING hilarious, Billby. Original, unique, never heard that one before. Fantastic, truly inspirational. Now make me some SPAGHETTI!

"Right, like I'm trying to tell you, time and time again, NO FUCKING HANDS!" Billby roared, shaking the room, the walls, the ceiling started to wobble and plaster cracked and fell and—

"Prawn! Settle down!"

Deep, long breath. Sat on the sofa, clutching Billby tight. Stared at the glass jar on the counter, full of uncooked spaghetti. I didn't want it anymore. I didn't want much of anything anymore, other than sleep.

Chapter 20 - Yes

Took down two paracetamol, slumped into the sofa with a protein bar.

"Hey, champ," Billby gently said. "Feel any better?"

"Not sure. What happened yesterday? We were going to Sammy's flat, and... it's fuzzy."

"We went. Try to recall the cult images, the blood, the—wait, scratch that last part."

... Blood?

"What about Sophie?"

Billby almost seemed to frown. "Sorry, Prawn. She's ditched you. We're on our own now."

Heart sunk. Tears welled. Smile died.

That's... she wouldn't. She couldn't.

"She did."

I could call Billby many things. A pain in my arse. A headache. A loveable rogue. A teddy bear.

But never a liar.

Didn't feel hungry anymore. Rest of the protein bar, in the bin, like my will to live. Flashes of a yellow cable—

"No. Don't go there. We are NEVER going there. Do you understand?"

I... I do. I do.

Checked my phone. Nothing from Sophie. Nothing from poetry group. Nothing from anyone.

Guild server. Nothing.

Work? Nope. Seems I'd got two weeks' holiday, that I barely remember booking.

No Sophie, no group, no... no cult. NO CULT.

"Now hold on—"

What the FUCK do you mean hold on, Billby? There were... there were pictures. But I—

"It was... compelling. Sorry, Prawn."

Compelling? She was crazy! She was naked, stacking water bottles and researching cultists online!

"Pictures. Robes. Dagger," Billby didn't say.

No. No, no, no, no. Not fudging buying this. I can't. Can I? No!

"You may have to."

Can't. Won't. Just a block of flats. Just a poetry club. Just—

"Just, just, just. We've been over this, Prawn."

Yeah. We have. But it doesn't mean you had a point then, or now.

I'm recalling something. You wanted me out of that flat. Why?

"Didn't."

Yeah, you did. You pulled me out of there. What did I see?

"We overstayed. All the evidence—"

NO! What. Did. I. SEE!

"Too late."

What? What do you mean too late? What do you... what did you do?

"Trust me. Have I ever let you down? I keep you safe."

Safe. Funny word, safe. Because I look around my flat—empty, stark. No pictures on the walls, no paintings or wallpaper. Nothing special or unique about this place at all.

"Minimalist. Feng shui."

Bullshit. Fuck off, Billby.

"Language. You're grounded."

You're a fucking teddy bear. How are you gonna ground me exactly?

"Good point, honestly. You are being a bit of a prat though, mate."

Am I? Am I.

Is it being a bit of a prat to objectify my neighbour? Push her away every time she tries to connect with me?

Is it being a bit of a prat to turn a fucking POETRY CLUB into a cult? Bear the Word? Seriously?

Is it... is it being a bit of a prat to poison everything and everyone I touch? Am I safe or alone right now, Billby?

"Yes."

Like I thought. Never known you to lie. But does that mean you can't, or haven't, or wouldn't?

"If it meant protecting you, I absolutely would."

Yeah. But what does protecting me look like, Billby? Does it look like keeping me so isolated I can't even risk getting into danger? Does it look like avoiding life from a fear of death?

"Yes."

Well... can't be doing with it anymore. I'm LONELY, Billby.

"You have me! You always have."

You're a FUCKING TEDDY BEAR! You can't hold me when I cry. You can't cheer for me when I win. You can't build a life, a future, a—

"Ungrateful. INSOLENT."

No! You... you don't love me.

"Of course I love you, Prawn. Why else would I be here?"

Couldn't honestly answer that. Couldn't bear to think of that time, that horrible... lifeless—

"No. Enough. Safe."

But I'm not, am I, Billby? I'm lonely. I'm miserable. I'm broken.

Billby didn't reply. Just stared at me with his hollow, lifeless furry face. Just a teddy bear.

I need to see her. I need to knock on her door and tell her that I'm madly, hopelessly in lo—

"No. Too late. Sorry, Prawn."

It's... it's never too late.

Swallowed hard, sprung to my feet. Door open, straight out into the hallway. Stepped over, knocked.

Knocked again.

Knocked again.

"Go away, Prawn," Sophie muttered from behind the door.

"Sophie, please. Please hear me out. I love you, Sophie."

Silence. Seconds stretched. Heart sank. More silence.

"Come on, kiddo. Time to go home," Billby whispered softly.

Chapter 21 - Prawn

Stared at his little furry face. Slumped on my sofa, eyes red and raw. Had no tears left to give.

Phone still hadn't buzzed. Nobody, nothing.

The guild had moved on to their next game already. Barely had a chance to heist my first space station and they'd already moved on.

Poetry club cancelled in the wake of Sammy. Tragic, really.

"They got her, Prawn. They can get you."

Fuck off, Billby. Just fuck off.

"You know I'm right."

I did. I don't anymore. I don't know right from left right now.

"That was unintentionally pretty funny, Prawn," Billby chuckled.

Cracked a small smile. Life wasn't all bad. Wasn't really life either though, was it.

Shut everyone out. Pushed Sophie away—

"No. Not giving you that. She LEFT you."

Did she, though, Billby? Or did you roar at her when she asked me to leave the flat?

Yeah.

Thought so.

Your silence speaks volumes, my darling little teddy bear. You push Sophie away, poison every relationship

I've got and tell me I'm responsible for it. You blame me for your isolation tactics.

"Safe."

Safety isn't life, Billby. Am I safe right now, or alone?

"Yes. Already told you that."

You did. But you don't see a problem with it?

"Got each other. What more do we need?"

Something. ANYTHING. I can't spend the rest of my life under the thumb of a fudging teddy bear.

"Paw."

Semantics.

Still. You... you gotta go.

"Wait... what?"

I can't do this anymore. You... you broke me. Poisoned me. I'm done.

"I keep you safe—"

Do you? Or do you keep me alone?

"Yes!"

Exactly. It's all the same to you. You can't tell the difference.

"There isn't one."

Yes, Billby. There is. But you'll never let me find that out whilst you're here. You have to go.

"Go where?"

Don't know. But you can't be here. I... I'm taking you to the garden. I'm burying you.

"Seriously? You're going to bury your teddy bear in the back garden? That's your plan?"

Yeah. I need you to go. And you're never going to leave me, are you?

"No. I promised you I wouldn't. I keep you safe."

I frowned. You do. And if I bury you—

"Nothing will stop it. You'll have to face it alone. I can't keep it away if you bury me. Please, Prawn, think this over. You don't want to do this."

I... what I want? You want to know what I want? I want to NOT BE TOLD WHAT I WANT BY A FUCKING TEDDY BEAR!

Furiously dug my way into the back garden with a spade I grabbed from the downstairs cupboard. Midnight, stars accusing me, bitter chill biting me, Billby staring at me as I dig.

Oh, no daggers or robes, by the way. Cleaning supplies. Nice and mundane, like poetry club.

"Like murder?" Billby didn't suggest.

She wasn't murdered, Billby.

"The blood. The pictures. The—"

STOP IT!

"Stop burying me. Take me home. I keep you safe."

You keep me alone.

"Same thing."

And that is exactly why I'm doing this.

"You can already hear it, can't you? Calling you from the drawer in your office. Can't sit me on the desk like a shield if you bury me, Prawn."

Nope. Ignoring you. Digging. Ugh, the air out here is so crisp, so fresh. My lungs hurt.

"Fine. Bury me. The silence will deafen you. You'll be back. You won't last the night."

Fuck you, Billby.

"Can't. Teddy bear, remember."

Yeah. How could I forget. You cost me everything, Billby.

I... I love her, Billby. And you poisoned it. You—

"Cult recruiter."

There is no FUCKING CULT, BILLBY!

You poison me to keep me alone. You poison everything.

"Some medicines look like poison to a closed mind."

Not listening. Still digging. About deep enough now. So why can't I let you go? Feels like you're... glued to my hand almost.

"Because you don't really want to do this. You want to go home, cuddle your bear, play your game."

What game, Billby? They all moved on already. Not even Badger bothers to message me anymore.

"Who wants to be badgered anyway? It means annoying, mate."

Joke didn't land, Billby. Sorry. Even if it had, I'm still doing this.

"You can try. Won't last the night. You'll beg me to come back."

No. I won't.

Chucked Billby into the hole I dug, feeling the world close around me. Every shadow, every flickering light—my heart skipped a beat.

"Think I'll make friends with some earthworms down here? Sure hope they don't eat fur."

Not listening, Billby.

"Never do, do you? I've had to fight against you every step of the way. Stubborn, just like he was."

You keep Tim OUT of this.

"You're the one bringing him up. Not the one stringing him up, though. Did that himself."

How could—why would—

Tears rolled down my cheeks furiously, bitter in the chill of night. Almost fully covered Billby in dirt now. This was it.

"Good luck, Prawn. You'll need it."

Silence. Nothing but the occasional passing car, the rustling of the leaves. I needed to get back inside.

Sat in my flat, shovel back in the storage cupboard first. Stared at the telly, pretending I couldn't hear it.

But I could.

"Prawn."

Chapter 22 - Prawn

Didn't sleep a wink.

"Prawn."

Nope. Can't hear it.

"Prawn."

Nope! Cables don't talk.

I was clearly hungry. Spicy prawn? Maybe some king prawn special fried rice. Delicious.

"Prawn."

Yeah. Clearly need to eat.

Could always order a pizza. That always goes swimmingly. Fudge.

Heart sank. Miss her eyes. Her smile. Her little text messages, her company, just... miss her.

Haven't tried texting her. Haven't tried visiting again. I... I can't believe what a fool I've been.

Might have driven away everyone.

Phone buzzed.

Karen: "Hey, all. Know it's been sad here lately, after Sammy died. Is anyone up for poetry club?"

Somehow, I didn't feel welcome. But maybe that's exactly why I should go.

"Yes. Writing my own poem."

I text that back.

Ali: "Of course."

Denise: "Sorry, we're not coming for this one."

Nothing from Sophie. I had half a mind to charge round there again, try to reach her.

Fuck it. What else do I have left to lose?

Steeled myself, took a deep breath. Hallway, stretching and twisting in front of me as I opened the door. Wait—Sophie?

"Hi, Prawn," Sophie said softly, stood at my door. "Can I come in?"

I nodded, stepping aside. She sat on the sofa, offering me a wounded smile.

"You scared me, when we were staring at those monitors together. Felt like I lost you. And then you... then you told me something."

If my chest got any tighter it might burst. She's come here to shatter my heart, gently, but at least she's come to talk to me again. Small victories.

"I longed to hear that from you. I was starting to think you just didn't see me that way. There were times it almost felt like you were pushing me away."

I swallowed hard, and sat a respectable distance from her on the sofa.

"I was. I did," I freely admitted. "I guess I... wasn't seeing things clearly."

Sophie smiled just a tad. "I'll say. It felt like you were someone else. But you seem different today. Sad, like a piece of you is missing."

"Prawn."

Ah. Not the cable. I heard him, just about, but his face was full of dirt.

"Well, um, Sophie? I, uh, I'm—I meant it. I meant it. Every word."

"I love you too, Prawn."

Right. That happened. Or did it? Am I hallucinating this? Is she still sat in her flat, ignoring me right now, waiting—

"But."

Oh. Oh no. Oh fudge. But. But what?

"I think we need to go on a real date, Prawn. See who we are, sat across from each other, candlelight dinner. What do you say?"

Fudge. I frowned deep. There's... no way. But I need this. I want this. I'll... figure it out. I'll find a way. For her, I'll do it.

"Uh, yep. Love to. Yep!" I cheerfully responded.

"Now come on. We got a poetry club to go to, don't we? And you're taking me on a date this weekend, mister, so be ready!" Sophie looked around the room, smile dimming. "Say, where's Billby?"

Chapter 23 - Prawn

"Um... he's in the garden."

Sophie didn't talk. Didn't judge. Just sat and waited for me to explain. Wasn't sure how. Grown man, tears falling down his face as his aching muscles heaved dirt over his teddy bear. What do I even say?

"Truth," I didn't hear Billby think from the garden.

Think I'd best just get my cards out. Show my cards? No, that's not it. Show my hand? She can see both of them shaking like lemons, so that's not it. How do lemons shake, anyway?

"Stalling," I imagined Billby would mock. Wouldn't be a liar either, would he. Fudge.

"Buried him out there. Um, I just, I needed him to leave me alone."

Sophie stared at me. I could almost see the cogs turning. Did she think I was insane? Maybe still thought I was a cult leader.

Actually no, think that ship has well and truly sailed. Maybe.

"He never once left your side. Weird to see you without him," Sophie said finally. "Sure you're OK with him gone, Prawn?"

"Prawn."

I honestly wasn't sure. Heart raced, staring at my office door. Glow from under the door, red, pulsing.

"Prawn."

"Prawn?" Sophie gently shook me. "You seemed troubled. What's going on?"

Clenched my fists. Guess I had to tell her. Can't just bear this burden alone forever.

Chuckled a little. Bear.

Bear the Billby. Bear the Word. Bear my heart on my sleeve, for her to hold or harm as she sees fit. Still, I was finally ready to at least try. Maybe.

"I talk. To Billby. He listens."

"Does he... reply, Prawn?"

"Um, s-sometimes. He wants to keep me safe."

Sophie smiled, though it didn't reach her eyes. "Have you, you know, talked to someone, Prawn? You're not crazy. I talk to my stuffed animals all the time. Especially my cheesecake."

Slumped back into my chair and gazed at her emerald eyes.

"I think I know what to do," I admitted. Hopped up, grabbed a pen and paper.

I needed to bear the word. Closed my eyes, pictured my bear and let the words flow.

I keep you safe when shadows call,

Casting red glows upon the wall.

The cable you can never know,

My paws upon it lest you go.

My love a lie, my shield a sin,

I lock the doors, I keep you in.

I keep you safe you shellfish git,

From cults and plots and other shit.

Problem is I'm just a bear,

I just can't give you proper care.

Push her away, keep you alone,

Don't even let you see your phone.

Gaze into her emerald eyes,

She ran away to no surprise.

I keep you safe and full of fear,

Wonder why you're even here.

Grab the cable, say goodbye,

Not a soul would wonder why.

I stared at the words as seconds stretched. Hadn't noticed Sophie leave. But the words were there, not by my hand, but by my paw. Truthful, honest, raw.

I had my poem. His poem. Our poem. And it was time to share it with the rest of the class.

Chapter 24 - Poem

It was time. Could hear the others setting up—first poetry club since Sammy died.

Still hadn't gotten a text back from Sophie. Must have been busy when she left, or still processing everything.

Didn't matter. Her love gave me the courage I needed to write the poem. And now, to stand before the others and bear my heart and soul.

"Sorry," I didn't hear Billby say.

Placed my hand on the communal room door, the others there already. The energy in the room was... solemn. Tragic. Looked around at their faces—nobody was smiling.

Gave Sophie a little smile and wave. Ignored me.

"Um, you OK, Sophie?" I asked.

"Sorry, Prawn. Still not ready to talk to you yet, not since Samantha's flat. Maybe later, OK?"

I... oh, oh god no. Oh fudge no. Oh fuck.

She was—no.

Left the room for a moment. Shook, tears welling in my eyes. Never there. Never shared. Never—never said it.

Pushed open the door to my flat. Pulsing red glow, bright, loud. Taunting, tempting, tantalising—

"STOP!" Billby commanded. "Poem. Go."

His voice muffled, weak. But I heard him. And I trusted him. Why in this moment, I didn't know, but it was time.

Pushed open the door, hands shaking.

"My turn," I said, all eyes on me.

Stammered and stuttered my way through the entire poem. All four verses. Stunned silence—not a word or a fart from the group. Nothing.

Seconds stretched once more. Pulse in my ears, racing, drowning. All eyes on me. So many eyes. Staring. Judging. Hating.

"My God," Karen said. "Peter, that was so, so beautiful."

"T-touching. Brave," James agreed.

Denise started sobbing. "You're so, so utterly alone, you poor boy."

"My friend, you would be honoured at the Ahmed table. Any time," Ali announced, touching my arm.

Looked to Sophie, eyes welling, tears leaking. Rushed up out of her chair, ran over and hugged me tight. Warm, soft, kind. Just like my dream. Just like my fantasy. Just like my fear.

"Oh, Prawn," Sophie mumbled between tears. "I love you, you shellfish idiot."

Tears escaped my eyes, too. I wiped them away but more came. I can't even begin to understand what happened here today, but I saw Billby's face, smiling, soft and happy.

Think it was time to get my teddy bear back.

Chapter 25 - Gary

"Took you long enough," Billby said. "Bloody freezing out here, Prawn."

Brushed off the dirt, panting hard from all the digging. Wiped the sweat from my brow, and carried Billby back inside.

Popped the shovel back into the storage cupboard. He didn't so much as peep a word or a thought the entire time. Got him back to the flat and scrubbed him clean in my sink.

"Feel like a baby," Billby didn't say.

You can be sometimes, dear teddy bear. But something feels different now, doesn't it?

"Yeah. I know what it is, but you're only just starting to see it."

Narrowed my gaze, studying Billby's soggy furry face. Hair dryer worked on fur too, it seemed, to my elation. Was glad to have him back, everything back to normal.

"Sorry, Prawn," Billby muttered. "Not anymore. I keep you safe. To do that, I have to go."

Go? Go where? You're my bear. You're going nowhere.

"I'm a teddy bear, Prawn. I'll always be your teddy bear, and you can always cuddle me. Not like I've ever had a say in that, is it? Inanimate object, mate."

Chuckled a little, despite my tightening chest, quickening pulse. He was building to something, and for once, I truly didn't know what.

"Yeah, you do. Always have. Time for you to wake up, Prawn."

Oh, that's so bloody cliché. Not with the 'this was all a dream' bullshit.

"Not literally, shellfish twit."

Oh. Fudge.

"I've saved a number on your phone, under the word goodbye. Call it."

Billby, I'm not liking this. I'm scared.

"Yeah, I know. But you are a courageous, beautiful young man. Go to the window."

Pulled open my curtains, light from outside hammering against my pupils. Daylight? When had I even slept?

I wiped the dust from my curtains on my trousers, and stared at the glass. Could just about make out my reflection.

I finally saw myself for the first time in I didn't know how long. Skinny, pale, a little gaunt even. Billby clutched in my left arm, unable to feel the weight of him.

"Years since you've seen yourself, isn't it?" Billby didn't say.

Maybe it had been. Not that it mattered.

"The number. Dial it."

Fine. I trust you, Billby. Don't let me down.

"I will. That's why you have to do this."

Clutched him extra tight, and stared at myself quivering. Enough of this. Curtains shut again.

I took a deep breath and called the number. Every ring stretched, heart pounding in my ears.

"Ah, hello again, young man. I appreciated you calling me. I promised you answers—I'm sure you all want to know."

"Um, who is this?"

"Sorry, isn't this Peter Ross Awning?"

"Um... yes?"

"Tracy Smith. You found my number on my sister's phone and called me, remember?"

I didn't. But Billby did.

"We got the results of the autopsy back. Bless her heart, Sammy had a brain tumour, size of a baseball. Drove her more and more paranoid and she never sought help."

Room spun. Billby caught me, helping me onto the sofa before I collapsed.

Woke up some time later. Dark now. Phone back on charge?

"Evening, sleepyhead," Billby stated. "She suspected as much when I called her. Nice to hear her confirm it. Well, not nice—fucking tragic, mate, but you get what I mean."

Yeah. Yeah, I did. But what about all the cult pictures, the—

"Photoshop. She was a graphic designer, some kind of artist. Found the originals."

I could barely believe it. No, I didn't believe it. Billby has kept me safe from the cultists, the 'Bear the Word', the cupboard and Sammy and the recruiter and—

"Tumour. Enthusiasm. Cleaning supply cupboard," Billby interrupted. "Come on, Prawn. It's time."

"No, no, no, no, no, it isn't, no—"

"Open the drawer."

"No!"

"You have to face this. Please. I love you. I... am you," Billby didn't say. I didn't say.

I thought.

"Look at it."

Pulsing red glow was gone now. It was... just a desk. Just a cupboard. Just a yellow ethernet cable. Simple, common, everyday object.

Tied into a noose.

Noose that my brother hung himself with.

Just limp. Just lifeless. Just grey. Just hanging by the cable, devoid of breath and life.

My burden. My shame. My chain.

"My creator," Billby didn't think. I didn't think. I thought.

I was... was Billby me? Are we us?

"Go ahead. Think of something random. Just say it."

"Gary the sentient lemon cheesecake," Billby and I said. We said. I said.

"The cable. Hold it."

Took the ethernet noose into my hand, shaking, crying as I did.

"Scissors."

Took it over to the kitchen. Pulled open the cutlery drawer, cold metal biting my palm.

I couldn't steady my hand, no matter how hard I tried.

"Here. I've got you."

Billby placed his paw over my hand, and together, we cut the noose.

Stood there a long time, Billby clutched tight in my left hand, cable in my right. It was quiet now. Too quiet.

Epilogue

"Hey, Prawn!" Sophie beamed, hugging me tight as I let her into my flat. "Today is the day. I can feel it. Are you ready?"

I breathed deep, exhaled. Smiled at her and nodded. I was ready.

We stepped out of my flat and down the hallway to the front door.

"Just a few steps. I'll be right here, promise."

The vortex twisted outside—gaping maw, mocking laughter and pointing and screeching and screaming and—

"Shh, calm down, Prawn. We're back inside. You lasted a full minute out there. Well done!"

A full minute. Caught my breath, propping myself up against the hallway. Big improvement from last time. Weirdly, it only felt like a few painful seconds.

"Picked up your prescription. And we're doing poker night tonight, too. Um, you want to stay the night after?" Sophie gently suggested.

I smiled wide. "Not yet, but I'm close. I, uh, I love you, Sophie."

"Love you too, Prawn," Sophie beamed, kissing me gently on the lips. Soft, warm, right.

"Well, come round now then? We'll pop on a film before poker. Play your cards right and we might not even watch it."

I had no idea what that meant, but I was just happy to spend the time with her. I hugged my teddy bear tight, following Sophie inside her flat and plonking myself down on her sofa.

I had no idea what the future held, and for the first time in a long time? That was perfectly fine.

Printed in Dunstable, United Kingdom